Teaching English in local and global contexts: A guidebook for beginning teachers in TESOL

Sarina Chugani Molina

Copyright © 2013 Sarina Chugani Molina

All rights reserved.

ISBN: 1495288757
ISBN-13: 978-1495288753

DEDICATION

This book is dedicated to my parents, Mr. Gobind Chugani and the late Mrs. Sunita Chugani. Your life experiences have nurtured in me the curiosity to learn about the various cultures and languages of the world. My husband, Larry Molina and children, Mina and Sai Molina– thank you for your kindness, patience and understanding.

To all of my students past, present, and future - your dedication and passion for Teachers of English to Speakers of Other Languages serves as the inspiration behind this book.

CONTENTS

	Acknowledgments	i
1	Introduction	3
2	English as a Global Language: A Paradigm Shift	9
3	Theories of Language Learning	13
4	Historical and Current Methodologies in TESOL	22
5	Macro-Skills of Language Teaching	27
6	Voices from EFL Teachers in Global Contexts	36
7	Guiding Principles for Teaching Practice	58
8	Conclusion	73

ACKNOWLEDGMENTS

This book would not have been possible without the years of teaching and learning interactions I have had with English learners in schools, community colleges, language academies, and community programs within the U.S. and abroad. I have learned much from my students, both graduate students who spent countless hours working with English learners in the field, and from my own English learners, who I have had the opportunity to teach over the last 20 years. I want to especially thank Marie Webb, Qingzhou Shi, Andreea Nicolaescu, and Miriam Voth for their contributions to the chapter on Voices from EFL Teachers in Global Contexts. I wanted to also extend a special thank you to Jaime Lenke, who spent countless hours revising and providing feedback on an earlier draft of this book.

1 INTRODUCTION

The purpose of this book is to introduce you to the field of Teaching English to Speakers of Other Languages (TESOL). When English is taught in the United States of America or other English speaking countries, it is often referred to as ESL or English as a Second Language because the language is primarily spoken in the country. However, because there are students who speak multiple languages, it has become more appropriate to use English as an Additional Language (EAL) or English to Speakers of Other Languages (ESOL). When English is taught in countries where English is not the primary language, it is often referred to as Teaching English as a Foreign Language (TEFL). This book has been designed to introduce you to some fundamental concepts of teaching English in both local and global contexts.

In the second chapter, I present the theoretical lens that serves as a backdrop of this book, which is approaching the teaching of English as a global language from a socio-culturally sensitive pedagogical space. The third chapter sets the stage for your journey to the practice of teaching by first laying the theoretical foundation that will undergird your understanding of the teaching methodologies in this field. Then, in the fourth chapter, both historical approaches to language teaching and current methodologies will be explored. In chapter five, I delve deeper into the macro-skills of language teaching, which include reading, writing, listening, and speaking. In chapter six, I share with you the voices of teachers who have taught or are currently teaching in international settings. Finally, in chapter seven, I share with you seven guiding principles and the cyclical tool of action research to guide your teaching embedded in reflective practice.

Before you move on in your reading of this text, I think it is important to share with you my historical, educational, and teaching journey that has undoubtedly shaped my values, beliefs, and understanding of this field.

This background has informed the theoretical lens through which I view this field and the selection of topics I find essential as foundational concepts to serve as a guidebook for new teachers in this field. Other researchers with different backgrounds and experiences may come to this field from a variety of different perspectives and angles. Therefore, it is important for me to be transparent and for you to begin to chart your own territory based on your own experiences as you venture into your future classrooms. The following is an excerpt taken from my afterword in the book, *Linguistics for Teaching English in Multilingual Classrooms*.

> My parent's native tongue is Sindhi, a Northwestern Indian language. Sindh was part of mainland India before the partition of Pakistan and India during World War II. After the partition, my father's family fled to the southwestern and central regions of India as did many Sindhis. In Sindh, he was in fifth grade with Sindhi as the medium of instruction; however, when he arrived in a school in the south central region of India, he was placed into a first grade classroom because he had no prior knowledge of Hindi and English, the languages used in the schools in India. He recalls this experience as trying and humiliating to say the least. At the age of 17, he moved to Hong Kong to work twelve-hour shifts in a relative's textile shop from 9 a.m. to 9 p.m., with only one day off a year for Chinese New Year's Day. He regularly sent money back home to his family as they had lost their family wealth during the partition. He spoke English to his customers daily, and learned Cantonese to communicate with his Chinese-speaking customers.
>
> My mother was born in Sindh, but during the partition, she lived in Indonesia, where her father had a business. She lived in Indonesia for eight years and attended schools there. She picked up the Indonesian language through her interactions with her Indonesian friends and the community. When her family moved to India after the partition, they moved to a southern region of India, where Tamil was the regional language of the people. Like my father, my mother spoke Sindhi, her native tongue, Indonesian, the language of the land where she spent several years of her childhood, Tamil, the language of the people of the southern region she lived in in India, Hindi, the national language of India, and English, the language of the schools set up during the time of British India.
>
> My parents had an arranged marriage and soon after their wedding, my father moved back to Hong Kong to work and my mother remained in India until my father was ready to have my mother and my oldest sister join him. The Hong Kong market was saturated with Indians in the

textile business, so when my father heard of opportunities in Japan, he decided to set up our family there instead. After a few years, he called my mother to come to settle in Japan. When my mother arrived with my sister, who was four years old at that time, she was so afraid of this new country and its people, that she pulled down all the shutters in the house for three full days and did not step out. My middle sister and I were born in this small village in Japan.

My father found two other Indian families in the neighborhood in Japan who were Punjabis, people from a region in Northern India. My mother learned conversational Punjabi from her interactions with them. She slowly adjusted to life in Japan, picked up Japanese, and found a small, but steadily growing Indian community about an hour away in Kobe.

My mother would attend Bollywood movie nights, cultural and spiritual events, and slowly became integrated into the Indian community that resided in the Japanese community. Through her daily interactions with members of the Japanese community, she learned to speak Japanese. She used the Japanese language in the day-to-day running of her household, when shopping, speaking on the telephone, banking, and ordering meals at restaurants. She also became part of the Japanese hiking community, further exposing her to the language. She preserved her Sindhi language by engaging in Sindhi community events and moving to an area within Kobe, in an apartment owned and lived in by a Sindhi tycoon.

My father worked in an import and export textile company and learned Japanese through bilingual phrase books, television, and through daily conducting of business exchanges. My father travelled for three months at a time on business trips to secure orders from international markets to be manufactured in Japan. He would export textiles in containers to international markets all over the world. These countries included countries in Asia (Hong Kong, Singapore, Malaysia, Indonesia, Nepal, India, Burma, Sri Lanka), the Middle East (Dubai, Kuwait, Saudi Arabia, Bahrain, Doha, Jordan, Iraq), Europe (Germany, France, England, Ireland, Switzerland, Spain and the Canary Islands), Africa (Egypt, Nigeria, Benin, Ivory Coast, Monrovia, Doula, Zimbabwe, Sudan, Kenya, South Africa), Mauritius, Australia, Fiji islands, and New Zealand. The language he used to communicate with his clients was English and was exposed to English in all the varieties you can imagine.

The Gujuratis, the Punjabis and the Sindhis, were three larger Indian communities that lived in Kobe within a half hour of each other and had their own temples and community clubs. The Indians all interacted in Hindi or English and when general events occurred, such as Indian new years day (Diwali) and community organized events such as the Kobe parade, these communities would get together and take turns selecting one Indian representative from each community each year to represent India in the parade.

When I was four years old, I attended a Japanese pre-school in our neighborhood. I was exposed to the Japanese language while at school and learned Japanese through my interactions with the Japanese children and from the teachers. I also learned Japanese through watching the local television programs. There were two private English-medium international schools within an hour from the Indian communities where the Indian children went to school. I attended a Catholic school in Suma, about a 45-minute trip by bus and train each way when I turned five. Teachers in this school spoke a variety of Englishes including American English, British English, Irish English, Russian English, Korean English, Chinese English, Japanese English, Filipino English, and Indian English. And within each of these varieties of spoken English, there were a full spectrum of accents. For example, I learned early on that there was no standard American accent because I had teachers from New York, New Jersey, California, and some of the southern states. Through these experiences, I was able to tune my ears to focus on meaning and understand messages in English regardless of accent. Likewise, I had classmates who were from around the world and English was our primary mode of communication with each other. We worked daily on negotiating meaning for mutual understanding.

When I would go over to their homes, I would hear French and my name said in a French accent, which I found funny at first, but came to love. When I would attend birthday parties, I would hear a variety of different languages, even Indian languages that I did not understand, but my ears tuned into these sounds and I began to differentiate and recognize these different languages.

Through my years of attending school and interacting with friends, combined with the steady emergence of American television (often shown at two or three in the morning), I quickly became proficient in both academic and conversational English. Although our schools provided rich experiences for learning English and understanding the different varieties of Englishes spoken around the world, it was often to the detriment of maintaining my home language and learning some of the other languages spoken by my peers. At our school, we were forbidden to speak Japanese or any of our home languages. If you did speak Japanese or our home language and were caught, you were given a detention slip. Such policies had adverse consequences for not only my sense of identity and the ability to express myself, but also for my potential to become a full multi-lingual.

In my community, we spoke in English when we communicated with one another, interacted in Japanese when we left our small Indian community and engaged in activities in the expanded Japanese community. At home, my parents also emphasized the importance of speaking English and discouraged me from speaking my native tongue, Sindhi. Because they spoke this language to one another and to us on many occasions, I am still able to understand much of what is being said, but am not fluent in my speaking ability. Another lost opportunity. Of course with India's booming movie industry, I picked up listening proficiency in Hindi, but with a lack of opportunity to speak it, I have not been able to develop my speaking proficiency in this language.

I began teaching English at the age of 16. Since then, I have gained formal training in the theories and methodologies of teaching English and have taught in a multitude of different environments to students of various English proficiency levels and language backgrounds. From these experiences, I have come to understand the complex teaching demands of teachers working in multi-linguistic and multi-cultural classrooms. This has now become our new "normal." In light of the expanding role of English on the global platform, the methodology of teaching "correct" grammar or what comprises "native accent" is slowly being shifted into a new paradigm, which honors the various Englishes that have evolved in different parts of the world and linguistic communities within English speaking countries as well. These Englishes have served these communities in communicating across language and cultural boundaries. It has provided a space for intercultural learning, business and educational opportunities and international friendships (Molina, 2013, pp. 95-98).

It is important here to also acknowledge the role my American school in Japan played in changing my life course. At the time in my community, it was very rare for girls to go to college. It was standard practice that the girls would graduate from high school, and through arrangements or perhaps in some cases love, the girls would get married. My oldest sister was exceptional in her academic work at our school so much so that our principal took the 45-hour train and bus ride and showed up at our home to convince my parents to let her pursue a degree at a university. My parents refused and my mother's one concern was, "What would the community think?" My sister resigned to this decision, but refused on her end to get married right away. She worked for two years and earned enough money to go to college. My parents had two choices. They could either support her, or disown her if she chose to go, and they knew they would lose her if they resisted. So, she went to the university, and now, she serves as a principal of a school. My second sister had no choice but to go to the University, though she was not interested; however, today she is a scholar, teacher, and practitioner of *ayurveda*, an Indian holistic approach to medicine. As a beneficiary of the struggles of my oldest sister, there was no question about my going to the university. By the time I came around to this crossroad, my parents firmly believed that the only gift they could give their children that no other could take away was education.

As I mentioned earlier, my teaching journey began at age 16, and continues today. I began by tutoring one-on-one and small groups, and as my qualifications increased, I began to teach in a variety of different settings. I taught at community colleges, both credit and noncredit bearing sectors. I worked with international students seeking to improve their English speaking skills to pursue higher education in the United States to working with immigrant and migrant communities seeking to simply be able to support their children in their schoolwork or communicate with their teachers, and improving their position in society. Like this, I worked as a part-time teacher in a variety of different settings and continued to learn about the practice of tailoring my teaching practice to serving the variety of needs and goals of my students. As I taught during the days in these various settings, I began to teach pre-service teachers in a master's degree program in the evenings about linguistics, theories, and methodologies that informed my teaching practice. Now, I train teachers full-time in this program.

We all come to this field from different experiences, but one thing I truly believe is that English is a powerful tool that can help provide voice to those who want to engage on the global platform. Our work is to support and scaffold these learners to reach the proficiency levels necessary to express their voice.

2 TEACHING ENGLISH AS A GLOBAL LANGUAGE: A PARADIGM SHIFT

In considering the direction of English language teacher education in both the local and global contexts, it has become important to consider TESOL (Teachers of English to Speakers of Other Languages) from a more holistic perspective. This paradigm shift has become important as we begin to recognize English as a powerful medium for engaging in the exchange of voices across the international platform. Though some may resist the idea of learning English due to the colonial effects of the English language and the imposition of the Western education system on the culture and heritage of its people (Crookes, 2009), many countries around the world are recognizing the importance of English for dialogizing in the global context and are reforming their English language education programs to reflect these needs. It is important for ESOL teachers to recognize this history and understand their position with a sense of critical consciousness, and approach teaching English as a global language informed by a "socioculturally-sensitive pedagogy" (Mckay & Heng, 2008; Alsagoff, McKay, Hu & Renandya, 2012). In this chapter, I present to you some research and holistic approaches in the area of teaching English as a Global Language.

Idealizing this idea of English as a Global Language could be seen as problematic, particularly where its future is concerned (Crystal, 1997; Graddol, 2006). Rather than English influencing the world, Graddol (2006) finds that the English language itself has been transformed by the world. For example, India has banked on its colonial influence of English and has rapidly generated a new economy based on the ability to speak English through outsourcing enterprises and other such ventures. Which English and whose English will be at the heart of Global English? This challenges the notion of what we consider to be native and non-native speakers of

English. Kachru (as cited in Crystal, 1997), includes the use of English using three concentric circles. In the circle at the center, he includes what many consider "traditional" English speaking countries such as the United Kingdom, the United States of America, and Canada. The outer circle, he includes countries that were former colonies such as India, Singapore, and Nigeria. Beyond the inner and outer circles, we find the expanding circle with countries such as China, Japan, and Turkey, where English is increasingly considered to play an important role in education, commerce, and politics. Based on this circle, whose language will our students attempt to approximate? Should you consider their choices in which English they would like to model? What would this mean for you as a teacher?

Based on the changing status of English as a Global or International Language, the questions I put forth above have become very important to consider. Moving away from the traditional understanding and use of the native-non-native accent binary, we need to reconsider English from the perspective of "intelligibility (recognizing an expression), comprehensibility (knowing the meaning of the expression) and interpretability (knowing what the expression means in a particular context)" (McKay, 2002, p. 52). The idea of what constitutes Standard English is very controversial; therefore, remaining within the framework of intelligibility, comprehensibility, and interpretability might be an important place to start. What is key here is that accent should not matter as long as there is room for negotiation of meaning.

In this next section, we look at some current trends of English language teaching as identified by Graddol (2006) in his book, *English Next*.

1. For many decades, EFL has been the dominant model for the teaching of English, but as countries respond to the rise of global English, the traditional EFL model seems to be in decline.
2. The increase in the teaching of English to young learners (EYL) is not just a new methodological fashion, but fits with wider reforms of education.
3. In an increasing number of countries, English is now regarded as a component of basic education, rather than as part of the foreign languages curriculum. A surprising number of countries now aspire to bilingualism.
4. During the next decade and beyond, there will be an ever-changing mix of age-relationships with skill levels, making generic approaches to textbooks, teaching methods and assessment inappropriate.

5. The learning of English appears to be losing its separate identity as a discipline and merging with general education.
6. Specialist English teachers in many countries can expect to see the nature of their jobs changing during the next 10-15 years (Graddol, 2006, p. 102).

These trends suggest that if you are planning to teach English overseas, you may find that you have been assigned to a classroom of very young children or adults. Within each of these settings, you may find a variety of different proficiency levels and needs. You may find that schools might want you to integrate English into content area instruction rather than a stand-alone course. As this field begins to shift, you might want to obtain multiple credentials and experiences, so as to provide you with the flexibility to pursue a variety of different opportunities.

In the final segment of this chapter, I would like to draw your attention to the position statement on English as a Global Language provided by the TESOL organization.

> The English language has developed into multiple varieties throughout the world, known as "world Englishes." These include the standard Englishes spoken in Anglophone countries such as the United States, United Kingdom, Canada, Australia, New Zealand, and South Africa, as well as local varieties in regions of the world such as India, Africa, and the Caribbean. The concept of world Englishes itself is rooted in the social and functional realities of language users in a particular context. Such versatility of the language allows nonnative speakers to use their own local words and expressions in their discourse, thus combining communication and culture within these world Englishes.
>
> English has become the most widely taught language in the world, and numerous countries have instituted English as a required subject for all students, often starting at very young ages. With English being taught globally for very diverse purposes, a singular or monolithic approach to the modeling of English is no longer tenable.
>
> As a global professional association, TESOL values individual language rights, collaboration in a global community, and respect for diversity and multiculturalism. In accordance with its *Position Statement on Language Varieties* (1996), TESOL encourages the recognition and appreciation of all varieties of English, including dialects, creoles, and world Englishes. In terms of language

teaching, TESOL does not advocate for one standard variety of English over another. Rather, TESOL urges English language teachers to make informed decisions at local, regional, and/or national levels, taking into account the purposes and contexts of use that are most relevant to their learners.

Given this position statement, it is imperative for teachers interested in teaching English both locally and abroad to do their homework about the context in which they will teach. McKay (1992) suggests, "While it is extremely important to do as much preparation and reading as possible before going abroad, there will still be elements for which you are not prepared, elements that can lead to cross-cultural misunderstandings and frustration. When such frustrations arise, perhaps the best thing to keep in mind is that as guests in a country, it is not the responsibility of expatriate teachers to change the host culture, nor the way that English is taught there; rather their role is to teach the language as best they can within the parameters of their teaching position, parameters which have been defined by the different contexts…" (p. 132). It is much more important to be asked to share your approaches as demonstrated by your student successes, rather than confront and challenge existing structures and approaches that might be in place in your initial stages of employment. Consider learning from the local teachers and the students about their expectations of teaching and learning (McKay, 2002; Alsagoff *et al.*, 2012). Perhaps forcing group work on students who are used to having the teacher instruct might create some challenges and discomfort for them. Learn about their culture and how you can integrate some cultural stories that are meaningful to them in the language classroom. Try to learn how to pronounce their names, rather than give them western names. Adapt teaching materials to reflect places, stories, and names that are part of the local culture, rather than bring in materials developed from another cultural perspective.

In this chapter, I shared with you a paradigm shift in the ways in which we conceptualize and approach English language teaching, particularly in the global context. Though this field is still evolving and there are many questions that still need to be addressed, it is important to recognize the changes taking place and adapt to this rapidly changing landscape. The chapter concludes with some suggestions on using a sociocultural sensitive pedagogical approach for teaching English in global contexts.

3 THEORIES OF LANGUAGE LEARNING

In this chapter, we will cover some foundational theories related to the process of language learning and teaching. While many theories are related to the specifics of language through the study of linguistics, the complexity of the human experience invites inquiry about the phenomenon of language learning from other fields such as anthropology, psychology, and sociology. It is also important to note that language learning is such a multifaceted phenomenon that no one theory can shed light on all of its complexity. Instead, this chapter will present a variety of theories that have evolved out of the quest to understand the process of language acquisition, but will leave you, the reader, with the task of formulating your own theory with a caveat that these theories will change through further research and your own exploration and experiences in the language teaching and learning process.

Before going into the actual practice of teaching a second, foreign, or additional language, it is important to first step back and consider your own understanding of the language learning process. This is because your understanding of this process will manifest itself in your teaching practice. This chapter will help you bring these often unconscious beliefs to the surface, so that your teaching practice can become a conscious, thoughtful, reflective, and deliberate process.

Behavioral Psychology

The behavioral approach to language learning can be best described through Pavlov's initial theory of classical conditioning, which involved a dog being conditioned through stimulus and response to understand that the ringing of a bell meant that it was time to eat. Before getting the dog to this level of understanding, the experiment began with showing the dog a bone. Seeing the bone caused the dog to salivate. Next, the experiment involved ringing a bell, which evoked no response from the dog except for a sense of alertness. At this point, the dog did not make the connection between the ringing of the bell and the bone, so in the next stage of the experiment, the bell is rung at the same time the bone is shown to the dog, which causes the dog to salivate. Over time, the ringing of the bell results in the dog salivating, where the dog is able to now associate the ringing of the bell with a bone. It might appear silly to compare a human learning a language to a dog being trained in this way, but that is what researchers believed was the way humans learned language. B. F. Skinner in his book, *Verbal Behavior*, published in 1957, took this idea of classical conditioning and did just that, but with the focus on what the learner does after receiving input on his or her output, known as Operant Conditioning. He believed that languages can be learned through the conditioning of verbal behaviors. In other words, through "repetition, imitation, and reward" (Gass, 2013). The focus was on providing activities and input to produce a desired behavior or linguistic output. Errors were seen as bad behavior and were immediately corrected. The focus of this approach was on the teacher's input and the oral production of the language without the consideration of the internal processes of the learner.

Structural and Generative Linguistics

About ten years prior to the time when the behavioral approach was taking shape in the language learning classroom, there was a comparative approach to language learning in existence. This Structural Linguistics approach was first introduced by Charles Fries in 1952 in his book, *Structure of English: An introduction to the construction of English sentences*, where he looked at the English language from a scientific perspective, breaking down the language into smaller parts and analyzing these parts. In terms of language learning, it became quite popular to compare and contrast languages and determine areas of ease and difficulty based on the similarities and differences between the learners first and additional language. The critique of this approach was that the focus was only on the surface structures of the language and not the deeper levels of language. For example, we might see the following surface structure, "While her daughter pranced around in the living room, the mother worked on her book." You probably already know that the original form or deep structure of this sentence is "The mother worked on her book while her daughter pranced around in the living room." This is a simple example, but you can see the complexity of language and the problems that focusing on surface structures alone might present.

Noam Chomsky (1967) criticized both the behavioral theory and structural linguistic theory for focusing only on the output and the surface levels of language. He instead, analyzed language from the perspective of how children learn language, which is also known as the Nativist, Mentalist, or Innatist Theory. He believed that unlike behavioral theory, which focused on input and output, children did not learn through imitation because of all of the errors that they made that he found to be a natural developmental process that all children go through. For example, have you heard a child say, "I goed* to school." or "I eated* my lunch."? All children overgeneralize this past tense –ed ending to verbs before they make sense of the irregular verbs and unconsciously begin to understand the patterns of language. He also noted that the input children received was not always well formed and yet, children were able to create novel utterances based on the poverty of input. He came to believe that children and adults to some extent had an internal language acquisition device (LAD) that helped them take the input from the environment, and register and sort it out in the LAD. He believed in a grammar that was universal to all languages, which he termed Universal Grammar. The errors the language learners make then are not bad behaviors that need to be corrected, but milestones in helping interlocutors (parents, caretakers, and teachers) see their developmental trajectory in the language learning process. It is important to note here that age is often seen as a determiner in the ultimate level of language acquisition, where children are seen to be much better language learners than adults. The critical period hypothesis was one such theory developed by Lennenberg (1967) that assumed the natural abilities of children to acquire language until a certain period, which he termed, the critical period. This theory continues to be debated given the success of some adults in language acquisition after the critical period, which has shifted not only the age range, but also the different linguistic skills that are impacted. For example, though adults can learn second language vocabulary better than children initially, they may never attain native-like fluency. The idea of native-like fluency also is a highly debated area given the rise of acceptance in the notion of English as a Global Language, where what comprises a native accent is constantly being challenged.

Constructivism

Cognitive Psychology further supported our understanding of the language learning process by expanding the language learning phenomenon beyond the LAD to general learning theories. David Ausubel's (1962) Meaningful Learning Theory or Subsumption Theory suggests the nature of how we learn through meaning-making potentialities within our minds. Contrary to the behaviorist learning theory, where rote learning is valued, Ausubel instead believed that learning occurs through meaningful integration of knowledge concepts, rather than accumulation of isolated concepts. New knowledge in this approach needs to be relatable to the learner's pre-existing knowledge base so that it can be integrated or subsumed into a new meaningful whole.

Jean Piaget (1970) is a cognitive psychologist who viewed learning from a constructivist perspective as well. He postulated that learning occurs through a process of formatting deeper and deeper conceptual meanings. Let's take an example. When my daughter was a baby, the doorknob had no meaning to her. As she grew, she slowly began to notice that the doorknob had some type of role in her happiness or sorrow as she observed it from her crib. When it turned, mother appeared, but when mother turned it to leave, she somehow disappeared behind that door. As my daughter began to crawl and get closer to the door, she realized that she could stand up and touch this knob, but still did not recognize its function. Then through many attempts, she figured out how to turn and then open the knob. The knob now had the function of giving her the freedom to go into another world (e.g. hallway). As you can see, the meaning of the word "doorknob" has taken many manifestations, moving more and more deeper into its concept. At first, it was something that moved, then it began to be associated with some emotions, then it was something that could be touched and moved, and lastly, it had the capacity to provide freedom in opening up to a new world. As meanings are expanded, old views are dropped or developed further to fit into the new schematic formation of the concept. In language learning, it is believed that through hypothesis testing or trying out of newly learned or acquired linguistic knowledge, one's conceptual understanding of those concepts can be deepened. These cognitive approaches also showed the importance of conceptual mapping through bridging background between the learners current knowledge or background with the upcoming content material in the course.

What cognitive constructivism did not really address was the role of interlocutors (e.g. parents, caretakers, teachers) in the learning process. Lev Vygotsky (1978) expounded on the theory of social constructivism, where the role of others was recognized in the learner's process of acquiring new knowledge. He believed that it was our innate nature of social interaction that drove our learning. A child learns language as well as other important aspects of being a human through interactions with his or her environment, which include other interlocutors. Through the process of scaffolding, the interlocutor is able to tap into the need of the learner by supplying knowledge or necessary skills to support the learner's development to the next level. He termed this space between what the learner knows and what the learner can learn, the Zone of Proximal Development.

Another constructivist view of language learning has been borrowed from Carl Roger's (1969) Humanistic Pedagogy, where the learners are central to the language learning and teaching process. In this pedagogical approach, not only are the learners' behavioral or cognitive aspects taken into consideration, but also their affective dimensions. In other words, this approach views the learner from a holistic perspective. This is a shift from the teacher to the wider context of the learning process, inclusive of both the student and the environment where the practice of teaching and learning is taking place. Teachers are considered as facilitators of the learning process where the primary agent of learning is the student. An approach often associated with this framework is Discovery-oriented Learning. Some examples of schools developed to promote discovery-oriented learning are the Montessori and Waldorf schools, where teachers are facilitators of the learning process. Other more contemporary approaches might include Project Based Learning (PBL), where students learn and discover through meaningful, relevant projects with the support of their classmates. Here again, the teacher's role is that of a facilitator or consultant who sets the stage for learning to take place.

Krashen's Eclectic Model of Second Language Acquisition

At this juncture, it is important to review Stephen Krashen's (1981, 1982) eclectic model of second language learning, and reflect on how his five theories are grounded in or resemble some of the theories we have discussed thus far. The following is a summary of the five broad theories from *Linguistics for Teaching English in Multilingual Classrooms*.

> Stephen Krashen identifies five broad areas that describe the process of acquiring a second or additional language, and serves as a good introduction to understanding theories in second language acquisition.
>
> Acquisition-Learning Hypothesis
>
> Krashen first differentiates between first and second language acquisition, where he postulates that first language acquisition is a subconscious process where children acquire the language through a natural desire to communicate and express themselves. The child usually is immersed in an environment where the language is heard and has caretakers (i.e. mothers, fathers, siblings, babysitters, teachers) who serve as models of the language and provide supports to help the child become a member of the linguistic community. In learning a second or additional language, theorists recognize that it

appears to be a more conscious process, where understanding grammar rules and knowledge of the structure of the language is often useful, whereas to a young child, such knowledge is often not meaningful in their language learning process.

Monitor Hypothesis

Just like the verb "to monitor," the monitor hypothesis is a theory that describes the process by which a person self-corrects their utterances based on the feedback they receive from their environment. When language learners overuse their monitor or self-editing system, they often produce sporadic, choppy sentences because they are so concerned about the "correctness" of their utterances. On the other end of the spectrum, we have language learners who do not self-correct at all and produce utterances with errors throughout. Over time, however, these utterances become quite difficult to correct and can become what linguists call "fossilized." As with dinosaur bones, which become fossils after centuries and are difficult to excavate, the same they believe applies to language that has been used incorrectly and left unaddressed for many years. Now, it is important that during the initial stages of language learning that the focus is on fluency because too much focus on accuracy during these initial periods can lead to halting speech and fear of speaking. However, as the language learners move from initial stages of proficiency to advanced levels, then focus on accuracy becomes important.

Here, it is important to note that there is a difference between a *mistake* or slip and an *error*. Corder (1967) defines a mistake as a slip which can be self-corrected, where the language learner knows the rule, but due to some type of stress such as time constraints imposed on their responses, they may produce incorrect utterances. An error on the other hand is one that the language learner is not able to self-correct because the rule has not been acquired as yet. These errors are ones that teachers should focus on and address through mini-grammar lessons by bringing these rules to their language learners' consciousness. Integrating grammar instruction through meaningful themes rather than in isolation can make grammar learning a more meaningful and relevant learning experience for the students. Ideally, we would want our language learners to be optimal monitor users, where they neither under use nor over use their monitors.

Natural Order Hypothesis

In looking at how children acquire first language segments, theorists such as Noam Chomsky found that they follow a particular order of acquisition, which often holds true in second or additional language acquisition. For example, children would often over-apply or generalize the [-ed] past tense ending rule to all past tense verbs before they acquire their irregular forms. For example, we would hear children say, "goed*" or "eated*" before they learn their irregular forms, "went" and "ate." Similar patterns of acquisition are also reported in the acquisition of second or additional languages.

Input Hypothesis

Just like we will not be able to understand complex engineering concepts without having foundational knowledge in mathematical concepts, it is believed that language can be learned when the knowledge presented is within the vicinity of the language learner's current level of understanding. The language learner's current level is represented as "i" and the level they can grasp next is represented as "i+1." In order for language to be comprehensible, it cannot be at level i+20 or 30. It should be closer to the learner's current level of understanding. Lev Vygotsky (1978), a Russian psychologist, described this similar phenomenon as Zone of Proximal Development (ZPD). Mothers and caretakers provide this type of scaffolded support to their children as they are picking up the language and help to make meaning comprehensible. For example, when the child says, "I goed* to the park today," the mother might say, "Oh, you went to the park today" with an emphasis on went. When the child actually registers this new knowledge and it is within their ZPD, they will slowly, but surely self-correct and acquire this irregular form. In the classroom in terms of language learning, teachers and even fellow classmates can often serve as models of the language and scaffold the language learning process for their students and peers.

It is important to note that in addition to the input hypothesis and working on the receptive skills, theorist, Merrill Swain (1985), postulates the importance of productive skills, which she termed the "output hypothesis." She believed that it was important for language learners to produce language and ascertain its correctness based on feedback from the hearers of the language. She theorizes that producing language has three important functions for language learning. One includes the possibility of noticing errors in their utterance. If, for example, the person with whom you are speaking raises their eyebrow or is puzzled by your utterance, you may do a quick cross-check of your utterance and find or not find the root of the issue that has contributed to the failure in communicating your intended meaning. In addition to the important opportunity for noticing one's errors, producing language or output can allow the speaker to test their knowledge of the language, what Swain refers to as "hypothesis testing." According to Richard Schmidt, when and only when one recognizes or notices one's errors, will there be potential for learning and acquiring some aspect of the language that has not been acquired thus. Lastly, output also serves a metalinguistic (thinking about language or linguistic knowledge and use) function in terms of helping learners think about their language skills and internalize rules they gauge from the input they receive.

Affective Filter Hypothesis

The belief behind this hypothesis is that low anxiety, high self-confidence and high-motivation, facilitates the process of language learning. Though research has shown that some anxiety can be facilitative in learning, too much anxiety may be debilitative. For example, if you were called on in class to answer a question, did not know the answer at that time and experienced some sense of embarrassment, then it is possible that you will never forget that question or answer for a long time to come. Likewise, if your losing word in a spelling bee competition is "broccoli," you may never forget the spelling henceforth due to the extreme pressure and anxiety caused by misspelling the word in a public forum. There are however, many more affective variables that may play a key role in the language learning process such as a learner's aptitude, metacognitive skills, ambiguity tolerance, willingness to communicate amongst other such internal and external factors (Molina, 2013, pp. 8-11).

In this chapter, we embarked on a journey of understanding the field of language learning that have been influenced by many different fields and perspectives. We looked at behavioral, generative, cognitive, and constructivist theories, and then Krashen's eclectic model that includes elements of some of these theories. It is important for teachers to take note of both the internal and external variables that play a role in the learner's language learning process in addition to the theories learned in this chapter. Before heading into the classroom, take some time to ask yourself these questions: What do I believe about the language learning and teaching process? What is my role? Who are my learners and what is their role? What are their needs, strengths goals and aspirations? How do they learn best? Thinking about these questions is important as your beliefs about how your students learn language will influence the way in which you approach your work as language teachers. In the next chapter, we will review some of the methods of language teaching that have gained and waned in popularity, but still manifest in our classrooms today.

4 HISTORICAL AND CURRENT METHODOLOGIES IN TESOL

Methods can be a problematic concept in itself if prospective teachers are seeking to have a particular approach with defined boundaries that they can immediately implement in their own classrooms (Kumaravadivelu, 1994). There are many textbooks and curricular materials that have been designed to "solve" all of our problems in the language classroom, or are presented as "the best way" to teach language. Now that we have reviewed the complexity of the language learning process in the previous chapter and the external and internal variability of the learners and the context in which they reside, we know that these claims must be approached with some degree of caution. In this chapter, I will provide a brief overview of some of the historical and current methodologies in language teaching that have gained popularity, and still continue to manifest in our language classrooms today (See Larsen-Freeman & Anderson, 2011 for a more comprehensive overview of language teaching methods). In reviewing each of these methods, it will be helpful to reflect back on your own language learning experiences and discover elements that can be traced to the various methods to deepen your understanding of these approaches. In addition, I would like you to think about the theoretical beliefs about language learning at the root of each methodological approach. This chapter surveys the methodologies that still exist in our classrooms today. Though we know that methodologies will continue to change, as will our student's needs, it is still important to recognize the contributions of the theorists that have come before us and analyze possible uses of these methods within our own classrooms if the goals coincide with ours.

The Grammar Translation Method

In my undergraduate program, the method used in my foreign language class was primarily The Grammar Translation Method. In this method, the focus was on translating literature from the foreign language to English. The discussion in class focused on the analysis of the foreign language text in English. The language skill areas focus on the development of reading and writing skills through the study of the foreign language grammar and vocabulary.

The Audiolingual Method

This method is grounded in the theories of structural linguistics (Fries, 1952), where knowledge of grammar is thought to be important, and behavioral psychology (Skinner, 1957), where conditioned responses through repetition of grammar structures and patterns are elicited often in decontextualized oral drills in English only. In this method, errors are seen as behaviors that require immediate rectification. The class is conducted only in English. Interestingly, this method was used during World War II to teach large numbers of military servicemen stationed in many parts around the world. This method provides a quick way in which to provide formulaic expressions that can be used in daily conversations. The language skills focus in this method is listening and speaking.

The Silent Way

This method differs from the previous ones in that the role of the learner is central to the learning process, imitation and drill were not believed to be the way in which language was learned, and the learner's first language was seen as a resource from which to develop understanding of the new language. It is similar to the audiolingual method in that it followed a grammar based structural syllabus. Gattegno (1963) believed that learners should attempt to learn language through their own hypothesis testing and that errors were merely demonstrating the learner's growth and understanding. The teacher provided silent gestures and mouthing of words to support the students in identifying their own errors. Only when it was deemed absolutely necessary, the teacher could help the learner by using their first language or guiding them in areas where they may be stuck. He introduced this method with specific teaching materials such as the Cuisenaire rods which are colorful blocks of different sizes used to represent a variety of linguistic concepts such as prepositions, stress, and words. These rods were initially developed for use in mathematics classrooms to teach number sense and length concepts. Pronunciation was elicited from the student using colored charts. This method appears to share many elements about the learning process from Chomsky's Generative Linguistic Theory (1967), Piaget's Cognitive Constructivism (1970), Roger's Humanistic Pedagogy (1969) and Krashen's Monitor Model (1981). Language focus skills in this method included some reading, but primarily listening and speaking.

The Natural Approach

Krashen worked with Terrell in developing this method to reflect the evolving theories in language acquisition that went beyond the notion of language learning through imitation, repetition, and error correction (Krashen & Terrell, 1963). Earlier, in response to the Grammar Translation Method, the Direct Method, as the name implies, focused on production skills through the use only of the target language. If students did not understand the meaning of words, the teacher would explain the words using gestures and visual imagery. The Natural Approach allowed the student to learn the language when they were ready. The teacher provided input that was just beyond the learner's current level of understanding through focusing on communication and topics of interest to the learner rather than grammar. Meaningful learning of vocabulary is emphasized. Elements of Vygotksy's (1978) Zone of Proximal Development, Chomsky's (1965) natural language learning process, Ausubel's Meaningful Learning Theory, and Roger's Humanistic Psychology (1969) can be seen in this method. The focus skills in this method was based on the student's needs.

Total Physical Response

This method first introduced by James Asher (1969) fell under the same category of the Natural Approach where the focus was on learner comprehension (Larsen-Freeman, 2000) and the teaching-learning process was in a low-anxiety environment. However, in this method, vocabulary and imperative commands were learned through actions or physical responses. The focus here is on developing vocabulary skills and learning grammatical structures in commands. Listening skills are emphasized before speaking where students respond physically to commands instructed by the teacher and later, the students have a chance to state the commands for their classmates to follow.

Communicative Approach

In this approach to language teaching, the focus is on negotiation of meaning through language within authentic contexts. The definition of what it means to be competent in a language spurred many discussions and discoveries, with the intent of going beyond the notion of language competence only comprised of linguistic or grammatical knowledge (Canale & Swain, 1980; Hymes, 1971; Savignon, 1991; Kumaravadivelu, 2006; Widdowson, 1990).

Canale & Swain (1980) described communicative competence as including four types of competencies. In order to communicate effectively in the target language, the language learner needs to use accurate linguistic components, such as vocabulary words, and follow grammatical rules (grammatical competence) in appropriate contexts (sociolinguistic competence) with coherent organizational patterns in combining utterances into a meaningful whole (discourse competence (Canale, 1983)). When there is a communication failure, the language learner should be able to obtain missing components of their system or repair the conversation through communication strategies such as gestures or circumlocution (strategic competence).

Because competence is difficult to measure, Kumaravadivelu (2006) preferred to use the terms knowledge and skills. He collapsed the various competencies described by Canale & Swain (1980) including grammatical, sociolinguistic, discourse, and strategic competence into two broad areas of language knowledge: linguistic knowledge/ability and pragmatic knowledge/ability. In his book, *Understanding Language Teaching: From Method to Postmethod*, Kumaravadivelu further elaborates on these two dimensions of language knowledge/skills as follows:

> [L]inguistic knowledge/ability includes the knowledge/ability of phonological, morphological, semantic, and syntactic features
> of a language…Pragmatic knowledge/ability includes the knowledge/ability of language use in a textually coherent and contextually appropriate manner… to be critically conscious of the way language is manipulated by the forces of power and domination (p. 23).

Communicative language teaching has many interpretations, but in essence, this approach has reversed the role of grammar from determining learning objectives and goals as a starting point to a role that is much more based on needs of the desired communicative activity. The starting point in this teaching approach is opportunity for language learners to engage in meaningful conversations within authentic contexts. Vocabulary and grammar rules are inductively learned or explicitly focused on by the language learners as needed to negotiate meaning in order to meet the communicative goals. For instance, one type of activity used in the communicative classroom includes the information-gap activity. In this activity, language is used for meaningful and authentic communication where for instance, students are to negotiate a study session time based on their own individual schedules. Jigsaw is another type of information-gap activity where groups are responsible for learning material and then teaching it to other groups. In this latter case, all learners are responsible for learning the material and then for communicating it to the other groups. Pair and group work are central in this type of learning environment.

As you can see, there are many approaches to language teaching based on what teachers believe might be essential to the language learning process. Many teachers might choose the most popular method of the time to use in their classroom, but again, it is important to really think through the needs of your particular students and the goals of your language lesson in order to determine the best method within your particular teaching context. Perhaps in earlier stages of language learning, students may benefit from the audiolingual method or TPR to learn vocabulary, grammar structures and to focus on pronunciation. In more advanced levels, perhaps communicative language teaching might be useful. However, if the goal of the advanced student is to study the literature of another country in its original language, then perhaps, you might find The Grammar Translation Method of value.

5 MACRO-SKILLS IN LANGUAGE TEACHING

In this chapter, I will present some of the research that has evolved in the macro-skill areas of teaching reading, writing, listening, and speaking. For a more comprehensive overview of these skills, please consult Carter & Nunan's (2001) *The Cambridge Guide to Teaching English to Speakers of Other Languages* and Brown (2001) *Teaching by Principles: An Interactive Approach to Language Pedagogy*.

Teaching Reading

According to Raman (2005), reading involves "knowledge of sound/symbol relationships (grapho-phonics), word order and grammar (syntax) and meaning (semantics) to predict and confirm meaning and structure" (p.4). It is a complex phenomenon that cannot be taught in a specified sequence. Instead, Goodman (1967) argues in his article, *Reading: A Psycholinguistic Game*, that the process of reading is selective and cyclical. The reader consults prior knowledge in understanding the syntactic, semantic, and phonological cues he or she comes across in the reading as he or she makes sense of the material being presented. The reader takes part in guessing meaning from context through the various cues and when it is not consistent, he or she will go back to rereading the same sentence to look for further cues. When meaning is determined, then this meaning is meaningfully integrated into the reader's existing system or schema (Ausubel, 1962; Piaget, 1970). This knowledge in turn will serve as a point of departure in the continued cyclical process of reading. Not only is reading a cyclical process, it also involves both top-down and bottom-up processes often simultaneously. Wallace (2001) defines top-down reading strategies as using the reader rather than the reading as a point of departure. In other words, the reader's background knowledge is central to the reading process where the learner can add new knowledge acquired through the reading to his or her existing schema. The bottom-up approach focuses on the smaller building blocks of language at the word and sentence levels.

Focus on one or the other would result in either fluency or accuracy rather than building both at the same time. Therefore, it is important for the teacher to recognize the needs of the students and balance the two reading approaches.

Pre-reading

Before any task, it is important to set the stage. Perhaps, you want to leave your students in suspense as to what the reading is going to be about and have them engage in a discussion in pairs about what the reading might be about based on the title and make predictions. If your focus is to help them organize the information they are about to read, you may decide to provide them with a graphic organizer (eg. KWL - a chart with three columns including What I **K**now, What I **W**ant to Know, and What I **L**earned; Venn Diagrams - two overlapping circles for comparison/contrast; Outlines - for organizing important information from the readings) where they can record the titles of the headings and subheadings and complete or fill in an area for summarizing important content and noting definitions of bold or italicized words. You may also decide to pre-teach some essential vocabulary that you have carefully selected to support their reading of the text. These vocabulary terms could be general academic terms they may encounter time and time again or specific terms that relate to the content of the reading. Before diving into the reading, the teacher should explain how the reading ties into the whole lesson and the subsequent tasks and provide clear directions for what the students are expected to do as they read the passage.

During reading

When language learners come to the reading process in a target language, it is often helpful for teachers to share their own reading strategies with their students including cognitive and metacognitive strategies, but also tools such as annotating and highlighting. Mark Roberge (2007) in his presentation entitled, *Critical Reading and Thinking Skills"* summarizes the reading process by providing the following guidelines to the students.

> Cross-check:
> - Does what you're reading match your predictions? (I would also add "How is what you are reading compare to your previous background and knowledge?)
> - Does the information you're gathering match your purpose?
> Reread:
> - When you've had trouble with a section reread purposefully.
> Continue predicting:
> - What's going to come next?

Continue questioning:
- What new questions is this raising for me? Jot them down.

When necessary, skip a word, sentence, or paragraph:
- Make a note about your confusion.
- You may be able to "fill in" the missing information later on.

Stop and review:
- If you're reading a longer text, periodically stop and summarize over what you've found out so far.

In addition to the graphic organizers or questions you may have provided students to complete by the end of the reading, these strategies will continue to support your language learners' reading skills as they move to more complex texts.

Post-reading

Depending on the goals for the reading within the larger lesson, you may want students to retell the reading in their own words to a partner or engage in higher order questions (see Bloom's Taxonomy) about the reading in groups. You may also want to present their stories in creative ways such as having them discuss and come up with an alternative ending to the story. You may also consider using the graphic organizers or reading journals with their summaries and reactions to the readings to support the development of their essays.

Literature Circles (Daniels, 1994) have become very popular in many reading classrooms as it shifts the focus from the teacher to the students. There are many ways in which to organize a literature circle, but in essence, in a literature circle, each student is assigned a role in the reading and is responsible for sharing his or her findings with the group after the reading task. For example, one student could share a summary from the reading passage, another student could share pertinent quotes from the reading passage and explain his or her rationale for the selections, a third member could guide the direction of the group discussion by asking some questions from the reading and the last member could illustrate through picture or graph the main ideas from the text and provide a rationale for the selection. These roles can be shifted each session, so all students have an opportunity to engage in each of the specified tasks.

Teaching Writing

In the past, and still today, teachers often collect writing assignments as a culminating product that demonstrates student learning. In the K-12 field and in teaching English as a Second, Foreign or Additional Language, the movement has shifted (and continues to shift) from product oriented to process oriented. In the process oriented approach, explicit instruction and support is provided for developing writers as they connect their writing with other reading or listening activities from its conception to its production.

Pre-writing
Before engaging in any activity, it is important for students to know the purpose of the task, the audience or receiver of the information after the completion of the task, and the way in which the task fits into the larger lesson. During the pre-writing process, it is important for the teacher to deconstruct the writing prompt and make sure that the students have the background knowledge necessary to address the prompt. Students can be provided readings, watch videos related to the topic or engage in their own research about the topic and record their notes in a graphic organizer. You can have them engage in classroom discussions where they can take notes on the variety of information resources provided by their classmates. At this time, you may also want to provide students with necessary cohesive devices such as signal words and transition sentences they can use for their particular writing assignment. For example, for process essays, you might want to teach them chronological or sequential signal words such as first, next, and finally. For comparison and contrast paragraphs or essays, signal words and phrases such as similarly, on the other hand, though, unlike, and different from might be useful.

During-writing
This stage of the writing process involves several steps including drafting, revising and proofreading.

Drafting

After understanding the prompt and organizing their ideas, students can immediately begin to write their response without consideration of the spelling or mechanics of their writing. They can use this free-writing as an initial draft if they are fairly advanced and workshop this draft to its final form. If your students are just learning about constructing written forms in the target language, you may want to begin by teaching your students how to write a topic sentence, body paragraph with supporting details and a concluding sentence. After students learn how to write a paragraph, you may want to show them how to extend the paragraph into an essay. In writing an introduction, you may introduce them to the concept of "hook," where the first sentence "hooks" the reader, providing background information to their essay, and writing a thesis statement. Then, you might want to show them how to go about supporting their claims with evidence from the text within the main body of the essay. When students are ready to conclude their essays, you may want to ask them to summarize their essays and leave the reader with their final thoughts. After pieces of the essay are assembled together, it will be important to teach them about transition sentences to provide cohesion to the whole essay. Transition sentences can be the concluding sentence of the previous paragraph that not only concludes the main ideas of the previous paragraph, but also includes an introduction of what is to come in the next paragraph.

Revising

In the revision process, students should focus on the main ideas and not on the grammatical or mechanical aspects of their writing. You may want to have writing conferences with them where you focus on helping them to clarify and organize their ideas. This might be related to clarifying the choice of words they used, the sequence of their ideas, and/or the development of their ideas. This is precisely the time where your students can negotiate meaning with you and you can pinpoint areas of individual needs. As always, remember to highlight the areas of strength before diving into a critique. Writing is such a complex process and supporting students to explore their identity and voice through this process is an incredibly powerful opportunity.

Proofreading

Though many teachers still are unable to see beyond the grammatical issues, and often penalize language learners for this in their assessment, it is important for teachers to sift through the surface grammatical or mechanical issues to the ideas their students are trying to convey.

Peer review can also be used during different parts of the writing process. It is most effective when the students have been explicitly taught the skill they will be required to review in their classmate's work. For example, if you have taught them how to write an introduction, you can ask the students to review another classmate's introduction to see if it meets the following criteria: 1) Does your partner's introduction include an interesting hook? 2) Does your partner's introduction have two to three sentences that provide background to the essay? 3) Does your partner have a clear thesis statement? If you have explicitly instructed students on grammatical terms and concepts, you can focus the peer review on just those ideas. It is important not to overwhelm the students as they are themselves just learning this information, so two to three areas of focus at a time would be most beneficial.

Post-writing
After your students put all this effort in producing a final draft of their essays, what comes next? You can compile their writing into a book for all of them to share with their friends and families. You can have them present their topics orally to the class. You can have them further research the topic and create a video project. If students write an argumentative essay on an issue the school is grappling with, you may want to invite a panel of members from the school administration to listen to both sides of the arguments as presented by your students. If your goal is to look for ways in which to reduce our impact on the environment, other students from other programs can attend these presentations. Posters and flyers can be designed to reflect the main ideas of reducing environmental impact as a class for the school to adopt. Knowing that their written work will be not only read by their teachers, but also heard by other stakeholders and used to design a school-wide initiative would make the writing process more meaningful and may provide more motivation for your students to engage in the writing tasks.

As an experienced writing teacher myself of over fifteen years, I have learned a tremendous amount about my students through their writing work. I have learned about the frustrations they have experienced in attempting to communicate in English and the discrimination they have faced as a result of their self-perceived lack of language proficiency. These conversations with my students have no doubt deepened my compassion and drive to help them explore and share their voices. These invaluable stories of their experiences and cultural traditions have transformed me as a person as they have become part of my story in as much as I have become a part of theirs.

Teaching Listening

In language teaching, listening has shifted from the perception of being a passive, receptive skill to what we consider an active process. As we reviewed the theories and methods in the earlier section we see the role of listening shift from the behavioristic perspectives of listening to imitate and repeat to the communicative approach, where listening became an integral part of negotiating meaning within authentic contexts. Pauline Gibbons

(2002) describes listening as a thinking process, where the learner is actively constructing meaning from the input. In other words, the language learner is more of a "meaning builder" than a "sound discriminator."

Therefore, both the teacher, or other environmental systems (interlocutors, television, internet/television video and audio) providing linguistic input, and language learners play a critical role in developing listening skills. When focusing on developing listening skills in the classroom, it is important to ensure that learners play an active role in the listening process.

Pre-listening
Before the listening task, teachers should provide students with an overview as to where this listening task is situated within the larger objectives of the lesson. When students see the purpose of the listening task in this way and a preview of what is to come, they will more likely actively engage in the listening process. In addition, the teacher should provide directions to guide their listening by providing for example, focused questions or a graphic organizer, where students can record important components of the listening task that they will use in an activity or class discussion after the listening task. This will help them concentrate on necessary input for the upcoming task from peripheral input. For language learners, if such guidance is not provided, the listening task from a movie or audio lecture could often become quite overwhelming.

During listening
Each listening activity should include embedded listening tasks if the goal is to develop listening skills. Language learners should be asked to pay attention to particular parts of the listening task by filling in gaps on a worksheet with focused vocabulary or structural parts or taking notes in response to assigned comprehension questions. Different groups of students can be assigned different tasks so that they can teach each other in the post-listening portion of the lesson.

Post-listening
Post-listening activities can include a variety of different features. For example, students could watch or listen to different views on a particular issue and have an oral debate. They can focus on different tasks in groups during the listening task and jigsaw their learning by teaching their part to the other groups. They can use the listening content in developing their own paper. They can work in groups and design a poster on the learning derived from the listening task. Integrating listening tasks within the larger lesson through group work will allow language learners the opportunity to listen to peers that provide input that is about their level or just a little

beyond their level and it allows for meaningful learning of the material through interactive dialogue.

Teaching Speaking

Spoken language differs in many ways from written language and hence, in order to be "competent" (Canale & Swain, 1980; Canle, 1983) or have the "knowledge/skills" (Kumaravadivelu, 1994) necessary to become proficient in the target language, it has also become important for language classrooms to focus on the features of the spoken language based on the important role that output plays in language acquisition (see Swain & Lapkin, 1995; Swain, 1995; Mackey, 2002). Output allows language learners to test their current knowledge, but most importantly receive immediate feedback from interlocutors on their production which serves as enhanced input so that they can then reflect on their production, notice the gaps, and revise their hypothesis about the language they generated. This ability to test and revise hypotheses of one's current linguistic and pragmatic knowledge of the language system is an integral part of the language acquisition process.

In many language classrooms today, you will still find that the majority of the output is produced by the teachers, with very little meaningful output generated by the students. If students do produce language, it is often at the surface level where the teacher asks the question, the student responds, and the teacher praises the student or corrects the error. This Initiation, Response, Feedback sequence (Sinclair & Coulthard, 1975) is what characterizes much of the input/output interactions in language classrooms today.

Group work provides opportunities for students to engage in the language learning process, where learners can listen to their peers in a less threatening environment than whole class interactions; however, implementation of group work requires some forethought and guiding principles. Gibbons (2002) provides some ideas on creating and sustaining effective and meaningful group work. Because listening and speaking are so closely intertwined, I describe the process of deploying speaking tasks in the classroom through the lens of assigning and sustaining group work.

Pre-group work
As with any task, the teacher must provide clear instructions, outcomes and time for the task. The task should be situated within the larger lesson, should be appropriate to the language learners ability levels and the task is

designed so that students will need to talk and interact in order to complete the task.

During-group work
It is important in any group work to ensure that all students have a role and are equal participants in completing the task. The teacher should also ensure that students have sufficient time to complete the task. All too often, we see group work where the teacher hands out a worksheet with 10 questions and students basically divide these questions, look up the answers to their questions in the textbook individually and tell each other the answers. While there is some value in the last portion of the activity, where the students teach each other the responses to their question, it could often fall into rote copying and reading. Instead, students can individually complete knowledge and comprehension level questions at home, but in group work, discuss questions which require them to work together to apply, analyze, synthesize and evaluate the reading or listening passages (See Bloom's Taxonomy, 1956).

Post-group work
Examples of an authentic post-group work speaking tasks could include dramatizing literature or poetry they have read, engaging in debates about a particular topic or participating in regular literature circles (Daniels, 1994) where each student has a different role in the reading process, but the groups come together to share their parts of the reading.

Integrated Skills

Although I have attempted to present each of the macro-skills individually, you probably have already noted that in many cases, all of the skills were integrated in some fashion into each skill area. It is important to base your focus skill area on the needs of your students, but also recognize that all of your students may excel in one skill over another as there is so much diversity even in each language proficiency level. Providing an opportunity for students to excel in their areas, but also be continually challenged in other areas is an important part of the language learning and teaching process. Integrated lessons provide such opportunities for your students.

The guiding principles, I hope, will provide enough flexibility to induce your own sense of creativity in the development of your lessons for your particular group of students.

6 VOICES FROM EFL TEACHERS IN GLOBAL CONTEXTS

In this chapter, I present to you voices of teachers who have taught or are currently teaching English in global contexts. The first piece is by Marie Webb, who has received her master's degree in TESOL in the United States, and has had opportunities to teach in various countries in Asia. The second piece is by Qingzhou Shi, an English teacher from China, who returned back to China after receiving her graduate degree in TESOL from the United States. She currently teaches English to children in Guangzhou. The third vignette is from Andreea Nicolaescu, who is currently teaching in a teacher training program in English language teaching in Turkey. She received her graduate degree in TESOL in 2010 and has been teaching extensively in different ESOL contexts within the United States as well as participates in teacher training both in the United States and Mexico. The fourth vignette is from Miriam Voth, a graduate student in TESOL with previous teaching experience in China. I have included each of their written pieces in their original form to preserve their voice, with minimal changes for clarifying purposes and flow.

Voices of Experience #1: Teaching in Korea, Japan, and China

Teachers are always bound to make mistakes when going abroad to teach. I have taught in Korea, Japan, and China and probably one of my biggest mistakes is not asking about the nitty gritty details before taking on a position. You don't want to come off during the interview as a pushover, so you remain quiet and try and seem comfortable and cool right? But, this is one of the worst things that you can do, as you may be kicking your-self months after taking a position for not thoroughly and critically evaluating your new position beforehand. As I have applied to more positions overtime, the process has gotten easier and I remember to make a giant checklist of items that I have questions about and sit there crossing them off and making more questions during my interviews.

1. *Not asking enough questions*

If the interview is cut short, which it almost inevitably is, I make sure to e-mail back over my final questions or call again to get my questions answered. A lot of programs and schools are short on time during the interview process. They are brief and leave a lot of vital information out of the picture. One example happened to me recently while applying to The University of Macau. Because their University is expanding and a new campus is being built, they could not guarantee my housing stipend when I first signed my contract. I had to wait several months until I found out about my housing options through the University for off-campus faculty members. 3 months after I had signed my contract I heard back from the University with my housing package. Still, I forgot to ask if this housing was for the duration of my 10 month contract which I assumed it was. Little did I know that the University had only secured my off-campus apartment for 6 months with the hopes of moving me into the on-campus housing as soon as construction was finished. Because I was not nagging the office and administration about every tiny minute detail of my contract, I ultimately ended up with more stress upon arrival to the country. Uncertain if I was to be moved again, I could not truly settle in to my living space or purchase furniture because of the lack of communication between the administration and the University itself.

I also had a similar experience in Korea where I was told by the school that I would have assistance finding housing. They sold this as a plus side of taking a contract with their school since other workplaces teachers are left to deal with their own housing and hire a real estate agent. However, they did forget to mention that there was an exuberant fee associated with their housing assistance and I forgot to ask because I assumed that this was a perk of the position. Assume that nothing is a perk, and assume that anything offered will come with an extra fee until it is written in stone otherwise.

These are things that you need to be upfront with during your interview. You need to be detailed with your recent experience and expectations. If you do not share with your future workplace what you expect from the position and contract itself, you may find yourself wishing that you took more time to get acquainted with their position and school policies and environment.

2. *Not understanding that other countries are still developing*

Many teachers assume that because they got hired at the top notch college or school that they will have high quality access to the internet and state of the art equipment. This is often not the case and is hard to discover without visiting the new workplace in-person before-hand. A company or school may tell you that you will have access to projectors, computers, etc. but expect that there may be a lack of technology that you are used to living in the United States or other countries that have the latest technology. I taught at a University in Japan that gave me access to ONE computer in another teacher's classroom to do attendance each day. That meant that I had NO computer to use in my classroom at all and no projector either. Everything had to be done with a simple chalk board and white board and I had to think creatively to plan my lessons without any access to technology at all. Even today at one of the most prestigious universities, the internet is often very slow because of so many classes going on at the same time. Thus, I cannot just hop on You Tube to show a video in my class or pull up an article. I need to download the clip before class and save it to my computer which takes extra time.

3. *They may think that their recent teaching experience or recent program will apply to their new workplace.*

This is NEVER the case! Each time I have taken a new position I have had to completely re-evaluate the way that I teach in order to apply my skills to their program. No program is alike and each University has their own guidelines and curriculum. For the first time I find myself in a program that is not focuses on specific language skills such as reading, writing, grammar. Etc. but strives to align itself with the core curriculum since the courses are a part of the required core classes at the university. Instead, I have found myself learning to adjust to the new curriculum which is focused on academic skills and aims to help students succeed in all of their university courses which a majority are conducted in English.

4. *Do not assume that the country you are applying to will understand or recognize your certifications or degrees.*

Many schools abroad do not understand what a M.Ed. or an M.A. in TESOL entails. Instead, they are still asking teachers to have certifications such as the CELTA or DELTA. But, in other countries a CELTA or DELTA will not be recognized as a high enough certification for teaching or it may be a required certificate to work in their programs. Each country will have its own idea of the best certification or degree required for its program. Your current educational background may mean something very different in another country which is something that is often confusing for new teachers in the field. The field of TESOL is always changing and is relatively new in nature. Teachers that want to be extremely marketable for a position should try and receive every certificate and diploma possible to maximize their potential for securing a job.

5. *Not understanding the difference between language schools, universities, and teaching programs.*

There is a huge difference if you are contracted by a private company to teach at a school or university versus being hired at the school or university directly. When searching for jobs, I often find myself researching the top schools in that country and looking directly for jobs on their websites. I also contact previous and current employees of these schools and ask about their experiences working for that particular school via linked-in and online teacher profiles. I have never gone through a staffing agency or government teaching program, although if you do decide to do so, it is not a problem. However, many teachers find that when they leave a job in Korea or Japan they do not have high level positions that will allow them to move up within their profession. If you are teaching at a "Hagwon" or "Private Language Institution" in Korea, this will not allow you to secure a job at a University or public school in the states or U.K. Many teachers forget that even though they have been teaching for so long abroad and have learned how to become a great teacher within their school, they still do not have high enough certifications and work experience to get them into a job when they decide to return home. They will still need to further their education after these teaching experiences. So, if you are just going abroad for the experience a TESOL course or certification is best for you. But if you are trying to become a teacher as a life-long profession than I would strongly consider furthering your education ASAP to maximize your job potential and expertise in the field.

6. *Your style and experiences of teaching and learning may be completely different than that of your new students.*

After teaching in 3 different countries I see the difference between expectations of the student and teacher the most devastatingly obvious in China. Students are passive, and walk into the classroom expecting the teacher to stand in front of the class and lecture while they take notes and sit in quiet throughout the course. In Western culture, the students are required to challenge the teacher and participate in class by asking questions and contributing to discussion. This is something that most students coming out of High School in China have NEVER done before in their lives. These students need to be taught the concept of critical thinking. This takes time and will not happen within a month or two of courses. Students are EXTREMELY nervous to explain their opinions or even raise their hand and share an answer because of fear that they will be ridiculed by their teacher and classmates.

7. *Your everyday work environment may be very different*

You may be used to chatting freely in the office with your co-workers or sharing lesson plans and eating in the office. But, in a different country these common work settings may change completely. In Japan and Korea, teachers were often expected to eat each meal with their colleagues or students on-campus. Where as many teachers in Western society may eat alone, this is not seen as a natural or viable option during the lunch or dinner hours in many Eastern countries.

Your office may be extremely quiet. My first thoughts on teaching in Japan and China were that my work environment was extremely dull. Teachers did not openly collaborate with one another during their office hours, and I often found myself leaving the office completely to escape from my cave down in the cold and dark dungeon. However, sometimes the school required me to be on campus from 9am-5pm regardless of my teaching hours which was the case in Japan. Many teachers in the states can make up their own daily schedules around their teaching hours. However, while teaching abroad, this may be a different scenario. Luckily, I am allowed to work from any place at my current position in China. However, I understand that the local Chinese people think that if you are not physically in your office, you are not getting any work done and you may be seen as a lesser colleague for doing so. My advice is to try and engage is as much cross cultural communication as possible in your office as the locals may have completely different expectations of the work environment. Often a sterile and cold environment can be changed if your co-workers understand that you appreciate their input and social interactions in your everyday work life. They may believe that they are distracting you, while you may believe they are rude and cold. This is a common misconception between those working in the Western world versus the Eastern world. Do not be afraid to share your culture with others and do not be expected to conform or mold your own culture to a schools professional environment. Staying completely true to your own culture may not be possible, however you can go through your every-day life as normal as possible while staying respectful of the countries expectations.

8. *Your students are stupid because they are quiet.*

I can't tell you how many teachers fall into this trap. Upon my first weeks of work in China a teacher said to me, "Oh yes, the level 0 students are very stupid. They do not know how to write at all." Don't listen to blunt or mistaken comments such as these. Often times there are teachers that are INSTITUTIONALIZED and have NEVER TAUGHT IN ANOTHER COUNTRY so they are out of touch with reality in their classrooms. Their teaching styles may be extremely dated and their expectations of students may be extremely low. This is simply not the case. The students coming into higher level university ESL programs simply have never had the opportunity to engage in any kind of sharing or reflections. Many of them are taught to take a test and remember the answers to questions. This is the only kind of learning that they have ever encountered before. Teachers need to be patient, and give these students many opportunities to produce ad practice their reading, writing, and speaking skills on a regular basis. Teaching down to these students will only hinder their learning. Often times I will be surprised by a student that is extremely quiet and shy in the classroom when I read their writing. This is because I find that they are even smarter than the students who try and participate in the class. Teachers need to remember that ESL students are processing information at all times and this takes longer for some students than others. How much a student is actively participating in class may not be an accurate measure of how smart this student is.

Other suggestions for new teachers

1. Don't be afraid to leave a position early

If a school is simply not meeting your expectations, than don't feel obligated to finish your contract. Most schools will respect your decision that their program simply isn't meeting your needs as a teacher and isn't a good match. It is hard to find the perfect program that satisfies your needs and desires as a teacher. Don't be afraid to try out many different schools and settings and even say no to positions or leave positions because you just didn't feel comfortable working there. I currently know several teachers in the field that have changed programs and schools after only 2-3 months of working because they did not see the job as a "good fit." This is ok! Many new teachers feel obligated to stay at their position out of fear that their reputation may be damaged for leaving. However, if you politely explain your situation to your current supervisor, they are sure to understand that it is often times difficult to find a good match between a school and a teacher. Don't let fear or money stop you from finding a better position that will suit your personality, creativity, and goals. If the job isn't meeting your expectations, then just leave. The good thing about this field is that you are sure to encounter many other people that have done the same, and many other supervisors who will appreciate your decision to leave a program early before they start investing in you as a teacher. There is always another job out there that is waiting for you.

2. Don't expect to be on vacation all the time!

Many new teachers in the field think that when they go abroad they will have an abundance of vacation and leisure time. This is often not the case as you are overwhelmed with adjusting to a new culture, moving, creating adjustments to your teaching, fitting into a new program. All of these things take time and you may find yourself busier than you previously thought. Teaching abroad is not a good means for traveling. Yes, there are perks that you are closer in distance to neighboring countries than you previously were if you are from the U.S. But in general, you will be working just as much as everyone back home if not more. Because I am so familiar with teaching in the States it is much easier for me to create a lesson plan or conduct research in that setting. However, living abroad often requires me twice the time because I am trying to take into account differences in culture and learning styles that I didn't previously have to focus on as deeply.

3. Travel or visit the country you plan to work-in beforehand.

Many times new teachers in the field of TESOL are just excited to go to a new country and experience teaching abroad for the first time. However, moving to a new country is a HUGE decision that should not be taken lightly. Before each contract I have taken, I had previously traveled to the country or conducted a job interview in that country to make sure that I could see myself in that environment. I knew that I could live in Korea easily after spending 2 weeks there in the year before applying for a position. I also knew that Macau would be an easy place to live in because I had been and lived in North Eastern Asia multiple times, and knew that the European influence would remind me more of my home culture. Upon traveling to Vietnam in 2011, I knew that there was no way that I could ever apply for a teaching position there simply because I did not feel comfortable in that environment. For me, I need to be in a location that is extremely safe and provides a higher salary and middle to high cost of living. This meant that most countries in South East Asia were immediately off my list as their crime is much higher than countries like Japan and Korea. I know this about myself, and thus I take is into consideration when I am considering a country to live and work in. Knowing yourself and your living expectations is extremely important when factoring in a new job in a new country.

Voices of Experience #2: Teaching English in Northeastern China

English learning in Mainland China is very popular as English is tested in many important examinations required for all high school and college students. There are many programs everywhere with tremendous differences between them in almost every aspect. Therefore teachers, who choose to teach in China have to be very careful about what kind of program they choose. They can either choose to teach in the public education system, i.e., high schools and universities, or private programs. Since I was born and raised in the northeast, I will only discuss ESOL in northeast China here. In other regions, things might be different, but some of the concepts may be similar.

In the public school system, the schools or colleges usually hire native speaking teachers to teach listening and speaking. (This means teachers from the United States of America, the United Kingdom, or other inner circle English speaking countries). Teachers usually can create their own curriculum, but the final grade is mostly given according to the final exam designed by the school. Class participation and assignments don't count much, usually less than 20% of the final grade. This has caused a problem in class participation and student engagement in the classroom.

The situation is also slightly different depending on whether it is with high school students, college students with majors other than English. Most high schools hire native-speaking teachers to attract students to apply without really trying to develop a quality listening/speaking course. In universities, the situation is better, but I would recommend TESOL students to go to programs with a concentration on English as a specialization or major. These programs have more professional educators in the area, better teacher support and curriculum designed specifically for language learning.

There are numerous private programs and language training schools in China. Because of the exam-oriented educational system, the programs and students are strongly focused on teaching to the test. There are programs exclusively designed for passing exams such as mid-term exams, final exams, the exams for entering middle schools and high schools, Gaokao (college entering exam), CET-4 and CET-6 (two exams required in order to receive a university diploma), TOEFL, IELTS, GRE, GMAT, SAT, TOEIC, BEC, etc. In these programs, students only learn test-taking skills and techniques. Most of those programs are on the "EFL black-list" on most professional websites in the United States.

There are also private programs that are not for preparing students to take English proficiency exams, but most of the teachers in these schools are Chinese teachers, who don't necessarily have communicative competence in English. Thus, they usually use grammar translation method and have the students memorize vocabulary, text, and grammar rules. In speaking classes, the practices are constrained by a set of words, phrases and sentences prepared by the teacher. As a result, it lacks the flexibility of authentic language use. These private programs also seek to hire native speakers to attract students. Some of the native speakers they hire, have little to no teaching experience, and at times don't have any post-high school degrees. Most of these programs provide teachers with very few materials and curriculum to support their teaching practice, if any. These teachers often can't seek another position outside of the class or school to teach, and some programs even ask teachers to play certain music during the breaks instead of doing anything else. Because of the special EFL context, few students have the need to learn to use the language properly and develop their proficiency in the four language skill areas. In sum, there are very few really good English language programs. In major cities like Beijing, Shanghai, and Guangzhou, there are better programs and teachers. There are also more and more people, who are beginning to understand the importance of language use. However, in small cities, towns and rural area, most teachers and parents are not very well equipped with the knowledge and skills for language teaching, and consequently the students are taught only to pass the examinations.

As for cultural factors, I would recommend teachers to stay open-minded. The two cultures are pretty different, and most Chinese students lack knowledge of what the U.S. is really like. Therefore, there are many stereotypes of the western world that are far from reality in their minds. Because of the communist party's propaganda and the rise of nationalism in recent years, there is also some hatred toward the U.S. Besides, most of them have never received any education on diversity and democracy. It is best to try to avoid talking about politically sensitive issues such as Tibet, Taiwan, etc. These topics can easily arouse discomfort and rage among students. It might also become a serious issue where the employer has the grounds to fire the teacher.

The students might ask some personal questions such as age, marriage status, salary, which are considered to be private and rude to ask in the American culture. However in the Chinese culture, this information or exchanges are common and demonstrate care and friendship.

Eye contact is another important difference. Avoiding eye contact shows respect to the teacher or authority, which is very different from the use of eye contact in American culture.

The students tend to be quieter in the classroom and wait for teachers to pick on them to answer questions in China. This is considered to be good discipline and preserves order in the classroom. When students have questions, it is more likely for them to ask the teacher in private after class than in the class. Asking questions might be considered to be not very smart and quick in understanding what they should have known. Not taking other people's time is also a very consideration for Chinese students. The students might feel they are bothering the teacher if they ask questions. Moreover, teachers in China are considered knowledgeable people who pass on knowledge instead of facilitators, who guide students to find ways to learn by themselves. Students tend to want more lectures from the teacher and may not feel as comfortable with peer-reviewed activities.

When receiving good feedback or compliments, the students might not express joy overtly. It is likely for them to deny it as a way to show their humbleness. It is considered to be arrogant and rude to claim one's own abilities even it is true. Humility is a virtue in the Chinese culture.

While some American classrooms allow eating food in the classroom, it is considered rude to eat in the classroom in China.

I hope English teachers who choose to come to China read more about the Chinese culture and get to know more about. Misunderstandings usually come from differences, and care and preparation can avoid miscommunication from occurring.

Voices of Experience #3: Teacher Training in Turkey

I, Andreea Nicolaescu, graduated with a Bachelors degree in English literature and Italian from James Madison University in 2007. Spending the following year in Milan, Italy teaching English as a foreign language to all ages and proficiency levels convinced me that teaching is my true passion. After this valuable experience, I decided to pursue a Masters degree in August of 2008 in Education, Literacy, and Culture with an emphasis in TESOL at the University of San Diego (USD). In the program, I had the incredible opportunity of studying courses such as the historical overview and theories behind second language acquisition, various strategies and methods for teaching English as foreign or second language, cross-cultural communication, curriculum development, and multiple literacies. Along with my mentor, I also developed my action research thesis on critical reading strategies through a cultural approach and was provided with the invaluable opportunity of implementing my research over a 12-week span at USD's English Language Academy (ELA). At the ELA's intensive academic

English language program, I was provided with an advanced academic reading course for which I developed my curriculum and approaches to facilitating critical reading and cultural reflections. Since then, I have been teaching various courses that I developed at the ELA for the past four years such as Advanced Academic Reading, Writing, Listening and Speaking, TOEFL Preparation, Grammar, and several electives such as Culture and Art and Utopian/Dystopian Novels. In addition, I have also worked as an Adjunct Professor in the Greater San Diego area teaching content-based courses at Southwestern College and writing and grammar courses in community colleges. In the past two years, I have been teaching Analytical Reading and Writing to matriculated students at the University of California San Diego (UCSD) in the Basic Writing program. Also in the past two years, I have served as a teacher-trainer for in-service and pre-service teachers in Mexico City as fulfillment of their TESOL certification offered, a graduate-level program which is offered through USD. So far, I have taught Second Language Acquisition, Linguistics, and Methodology I and II, all courses which I find highly enjoyable and would like to continue to teach in the future as I find teacher-training to be a fulfilling endeavor towards the growth of my career.

Currently, I am an English Language Fellow at Kocaeli University in Turkey where I have been teaching in their English Language Teaching (ELT) Department courses such as ELT Methodology, Academic Reading, and Novel Analysis. Each of these courses I feel quite well-prepared for as a result of my studies in USD's Literacy, Culture and TESOL Masters program and my subsequent teaching at USD's English Language Academy as well as my teacher-training experience to the in-service and pre-service teachers in Mexico.

I would like to briefly reflect on my observations and experiences thus far with the student population here at Kocaeli University and offer some suggestions for anyone who would be interested in teaching at a public university in Turkey in the near future.

My students are typically aged 18 to 22, though there are a few students in their late 20s and early 30s as well. They come from a variety of socioeconomic backgrounds, with some working their way through school and others who seem to be fairly comfortable financially. Their English skill level is also a range, though Kocaeli University has an entrance exam and a preparatory class for students who are not able to meet the minimum standards in listening, reading, writing, speaking and grammar. Most students entering the first year of the program are at a high intermediate or low advanced level. Their main motivation for taking these classes is to obtain a bachelor's degree in English Language Teaching and most aim to be English teachers in the future. In terms of their language needs, the students need to first and foremost further develop their academic reading, writing, and oral skills and be prepared to communicate more comfortably in general English situations; some also need to improve their English skills specifically related to classroom management. Many students have had a variety of opportunities to read and write English to a certain extent but have had more limited opportunities to interact orally with English speakers. Thus, I see a need for learners to continue to expand both their academic and communicative competence and be provided with more opportunities to use English in real-life situations.

Since the English teaching program and the course load that is offered at Kocaeli University is organized quite similarly to the education program at USD, I have adapted rather well to my situation, and I feel that there is little to discuss in the way of challenges. One aspect that does seem to be somewhat of an unavoidable challenge is the issue of failing students. When a student fails a class, they are often provided with another chance to pass through "butunleme" or make-up exams, and this does not fit well with the type of assessments I create, which are often project-based. Students who fail from this then are required to repeat the class the following year, working on their own time, or taking the make-up exams at the scheduled times. I mention this only because from a programmatic point of view, if English fellows were better informed about these policies in advance, they could prepare for them better in terms of the assessments they plan and what exceptions they might need to make for failing students and repeaters. In my case, no written handbook of policies exists in English, and I continue to be taken by surprise by regulations that are only explained to me on an ad hoc basis.

Language can definitely be a bit of a barrier since aside from the university campus, actually, more specifically the students enrolled in the English teaching program, most Turkish people I have encountered thus far have very limited to no English communicative abilities. I would really encourage anyone coming to Turkey to learn as much of the language as they possibly can before they arrive and then keep it up after arriving. Several of my students have volunteered their time to tutor me, and it works out well; they get the teaching experience, and I get to improve my knowledge of the Turkish language and culture.

As with most other teaching abroad opportunities, including my current experience of teaching at a public university in Turkey, my advice is to find out as much as possible about the expected roles of teachers and students by engaging in some observations and reflections. During my first week of arriving at my university, I observed several of my colleagues' courses, particularly courses that I knew I would be teaching in the near future. I observed four different professors' courses not only to be able to reflect on a variety of teaching styles but also to see how different content areas might affect teaching approaches and students' behavior. Throughout my observations, tried to keep various questions in mind such as "how are the students behaving with other teachers? How are the teachers approaching their students, varying their instruction, and managing their classes? What are the school and/or the instructor's policies regarding assignments, tardiness and attendance?" Overall, so far I have not observed anything that I could comment on as diverging from what I have found to be more or less typical classroom activities. Two possible issues that stood out were that in one classroom, several students were checking their cellphones quite frequently while in another classroom some students walked in 15, 20, even 30 minutes after the class had started. I realized that before I could establish my own credibility as a teacher, I would need to first understand what my students have been accustomed to expect and approach the situation from there in a way that naturally fits my own teaching values and always through open communication.

Another slight challenge I have faced is the relatively larger classrooms here in comparison to the classes I had been teaching in San Diego, which typically ranged in number from 10-20 students. Here at Kocaeli University, an average class consists of anywhere from a minimum of 25 to 35-40 students, and at least initially, classroom management approaches had to be somewhat adjusted and fine-tuned. I tried to envision a more learner-centered classroom where I have modeled and taught the students to take responsibility for completing their assignments and class projects within small collaborative groups. As these students will soon become teachers of their own, I wanted to create a space where each group member was assigned individual roles and tasks to enable their group members to work cooperatively and effectively in creating a learning environment both within their group and for the benefit of their whole-class.

An aspect of teaching which I continue to value and find true regardless of the country or classroom is quite simple in nature. Students will respond positively if they feel that I am genuinely interested in them and care about their thoughts and values. One basic, initial way to build a caring relationship with my students was to learn their names as quickly as possible. On the first day, I learned that each Turkish name has an actual meaning and can be translated. For example, the name Nurdan means "made of light," Azra means "a garden from Heaven," and Rumeysa translates to "team of the stars." Taking the time to have each student reflect on the individual meaning of their names was so meaningful for me, and I appreciated that they were willing to share a personal aspect of themselves, while they appreciated seeing that I genuinely cared.

In planning each of my lessons, whether they are for my language teaching methodology courses, my academic reading courses, or my novel analysis electives, I always initiate a discussion by activating students' previous background knowledge on the topic and initiating a small group or whole class discussion. Frequently inviting students to share related examples and personal thoughts and experiences is invaluable, and somehow cultural ideas always become interspersed within all lessons. I set out to identify activities in which all of the students can participate in and select several approaches for each class session both for presenting new concepts and assessing and having students apply what they have learned such as through lectures, think-pair-shares, jigsaw activities, smallgroup discussions, short written reflections, and whole class presentations.

As far as overseas teaching experiences go, I would have to say that this experience has been a wonderful learning opportunity for me so far. Turkey is a historically and culturally rich country with caring and hospitable people. It is rather well-developed economically, and that makes life here easier than what I would imagine some of the fellows in other countries might experience. Our classrooms are new, also due to the reconstruction after the 1999 earthquake, and equipped with modern amenities. More importantly, the students, my colleagues, and other people I have gotten to know are well-educated and often well-traveled and open-minded. In terms of culture, the people I have encountered have been very genuine, open, and helpful in assisting me with settling in and discovering a little piece of their world.

Voices of Experience #4: Teaching English in China

Context & Student Backgrounds

I taught English in China for 4 years at Hubei Polytechnic Institute in Xiaogan, Hubei Province. It is a 3 year college where students spend the first 2 years in classes at the school and the third year is devoted to jobs or studying for an exam to get into university. Students graduate with a certificate in their program rather than a degree, somewhat similar to getting an A.A. from a two year program here in the U.S. The programs are vocationally oriented with an emphasis on practicum. As with many vocational schools, it is considered the lower tier of secondary education for those who lack the academic skills for University (and at worst considered a place for less intelligent students). Personally, I loved this setting. I liked the practical emphasis of the courses and enjoyed the focus on career application. One aspect of the school culture that I found troubling was that students were viewed as failures academically and often personally. This attitude came from the students themselves as well as the general attitude I observed in China toward the educational hierarchy. My students had "failed" the National Higher Education Entrance Exam by not obtaining a score high enough to qualify for a university. This exam, called the Gaokao, is extremely important in Chinese society and serves as a measure of worth in some regards. The day of the exam was described to me by many as the "black day" because of the high level of anxiety felt by students and their families. This exam was also commonly referred to as the most difficult experience faced by students in the education system and a defining life experience. I estimate that perhaps 20% of my students felt lucky to be attending Hubei Polytechnic while the remaining 80% felt they were failures who had disappointed their families, were facing a bleak future, and in many cases that they themselves were not very intelligent. However, what I observed among my students was not really an intelligence issue as much as lack of academic skills and effective study habits, mild to severe undiagnosed learning disabilities, severe test anxiety, undiagnosed depression or anxiety, or lower quality education received in rural schools. The cultural emphasis on academic achievement is extremely high, resulting in intense pressure on students to pass national exams and the connection of self-worth to these scores.

The majority of my students were from villages and small towns. Their parents were usually farmers, factory workers, or small business owners. For many of them, they were getting a higher level of education than their parents had had the opportunity to achieve. For a few students they were among the first of their village to attend college. Several had one or more siblings who had gone to work to help pay for their tuition so the pressure to succeed and be able to repay the family was quite high. In China children are responsible for caring for their parents in their old age, and in addition wealthier family members are expected to help support the extended family financially. For students who were the first or among the first generation to get a higher education, this responsibility was already starting to fall on them and they often talked about the pressure they were under to do well on exams and earn a high salary after graduating. For students who were only children, this pressure was also quite high since their parents were depending entirely on them. The most common answer to questions such as "why are you studying English?" was "So that I can get a good job and relieve my parents' burden." While this cultural expectation is generally high regardless of socioeconomic status, the majority of my students' parents had spent all their money supporting their education, leaving little or no savings for their retirement. While most students were able to manage the pressure, others were experiencing anxiety or exhibiting other signs of being overwhelmed. While I do not wish to paint a bleak picture or imply that all students were living under a dark cloud, I think it was crucial for me as a teacher to understand these undercurrents in my students' lives. In general compared to college students in the US, they tended to be more serious about their careers, feel higher pressure to get high paying jobs right after graduating, and already have people depending on them financially. This would be a little different among students at other schools or in universities in China. A teacher new to teaching English in China will need to investigate their own students' backgrounds, values, and goals.

The academic style and administrative structure of the school also took time to understand. It was not until my second and third year that I felt I was able to work well within my department and understand the intricacies of the interpersonal relationship structure enough to use it. Every institution and department has its own unique culture, however I think it would be helpful for new teachers to understand a few key concepts: the role of "foreign teachers," guanxi, face, and indirectness.

Foreign teachers, or wai jiao, usually hold a unique position within a school. They are usually not subject to the same expectations as other faculty (of course depending on the institution). Learning the expectations for foreign teachers at a particular school will be very important. For Hubei Polytechnic, employing native English speakers was important for recruiting for several departments so we were asked to participate in recruiting trips, on promotional materials, attend events, present awards, perform at holiday events, meet with city leaders at official events, and occasionally judge English speech contests for various departments. This would not be typical of every school, but Foreign Teachers will likely find that there are many extra requests on their time. For that reason, it is also important for teachers to set boundaries so that they do not lose focus on their classes. Unless a Foreign Teacher is able to speak Chinese and is able to attend faculty meetings, it will likely be difficult to find out much of what goes on in the department and school. This leads to situations such as Foreign Teachers being called 30 minutes before an event and being informed that their classes have been cancelled so that they can attend. It is important to be flexible and helpful to find people who are well informed who can help pass along information. My school did a better job than many I heard about. They had adapted to having Western teachers who expected to know information farther ahead of time and did a good job of letting us know several days before events or schedule changes would occur. It is worth noting here that frequently administration was not informed about events or changes until the last moment and were not able to make arrangements in advance (the power structure for information flow can be quite complex and when one is informed depends on position within the power and relationship structure). I frequently found out important information from my students before I heard from my dean. Again, this depends somewhat on the school and department as well as personal communication styles of the staff and administrators, though these are things I have heard from many other teachers in other schools as well.

As mentioned briefly above, relationship status plays a role in communication. It also has much broader implications. In Chinese culture, the term guanxi means relationship. More specifically it is used to refer to strong networks of personal relationships that govern social and business interaction in Chinese society. A person is expected to build and maintain personal relationships with friends, colleagues, business associates, officials, etc. The status of relationship generally determines the success of interactions with people in each arena. Relationship building is of course an aspect of every culture, however the emphasis on personal relationships or connections in the professional world in China is much stronger than it is in U.S. culture – in most cases it supersedes professional roles. Relationship networks mean everything. If one is sick, one uses family or friend connections to hospital staff to ensure good treatment. Within school structure, Foreign Teachers often have a certain amount of influence afforded them because of their status. However it is still extremely important to build and maintain relationships and participate in the various dinners and events to network with faculty, staff, and administration. Time is also important. New teachers may find it more difficult to get information, permission, quick responses to requests, or additional materials. Returning teachers who have formed good relationships with faculty and administration will likely find this much easier. My first year, there was another foreign teacher who had been at the school for 9 years and she had high status within the department and school. She would sometimes make requests on my behalf when I had been unable to get any traction on my own. By my second year I had been able to establish my own relationships and had gotten used to how the guanxi relationship structure worked and so I needed this help less frequently. It is important for a new teacher to realize that it will take some time to establish relationships. It may be a frustrating process at first since the relationship dynamics may be quite foreign and confusing. It took time for me to stop feeling like people were irresponsible and unprofessional and recognize responsibility and professionalism were shown within that context. It is also important to note that guanxi is also the responsibility to take care of those you have a relationship with. My school took the responsibility to care for me as a foreigner living in China very seriously. They sent interpreters with me to the hospital, helped make travel arrangements, and always looked out for my safety and comfort – far beyond what I would have expected.

A concept related to guanxi is "face" or dignity, prestige, and honor. There are many words in Chinese for this concept, with mianzi being perhaps the most common. This complex concept is well worth researching before going to China. Although it is used in English and in sociology, the meaning within Chinese culture has greater depth and a much greater significance. Face plays an important role in relationships since it also carries the meaning of reputation and moral character. One's "face" is extremely important to maintain, or in other words one must maintain one's dignity and honor (save face). However it is even more important that one does not cause someone else to lose face (be dishonored). When one does something which honors another person or contributes to their good reputation, it is called "giving face." This is often done through self-deprecation, refraining from public displays of anger (with superiors or peers), effusive praise or compliments, and fulfilling one's obligations. These are very complex concepts that play out in many ways in Chinese culture. For a Foreign Teacher, it will be important to learn how to interact with faculty, administration, and students in order to avoid causing loss of face and to give face to others, the department, and school. There were several ways that face played a role in classroom interactions:

- Students sometimes told me it was difficult to speak English with their classmates because it was embarrassing – they did not want to confuse their classmates and thereby cause them to lose face;
- Students always answered in the affirmative when I asked if they understood instructions because they felt it would cause me to feel embarrassed and lose face. Only after we had established a closer relationship were students willing to let me know they had not understood;
- When criticized, students tended to smile or laugh rather than show their embarrassment or regret. This was sometimes interpreted by U.S. foreign teachers as defiance. However I think students were trying to save face and lessen the discomfort of the situation. Expressing anger to someone with authority over you causes loss of face;
- If asked to help another student, even if that help could be considered cheating, it was very difficult to refuse because it would result in loss of face to both parties and damage *guanxi*.

Again, understanding of face and how to adjust to the culture will take time. It will take careful attention and reflection on the success of failure of communication and interactions. It was extremely helpful to me to have Chinese colleagues and friends who were able to explain confusing situations and explicitly discuss cultural values.

And finally, indirect communication is more common in Chinese culture than in Western culture. This is another area where good research will be helpful. U.S. teachers tend to be too direct and become frustrated by the indirect nature of communication with administration. This is important because it also ties into *guanxi* and face since communication forms the basis for relationships. While it is not possible to fully discuss this here, it is important to note that time, attention, and reflection will help new teachers adapt and build intercultural communication skills. It is very important to avoid labelling the differences as "bad communication" because that will automatically put up an obstacle to successful communication. One thing to note is that among friends, it is common to be much more direct and refrain from using polite terms such as "please" and "thank you" which denotes the closeness of the relationship. Here too it is helpful to find Chinese friends who are able to explain confusing situations or give advice for repairing communication breakdowns. This will need to be a person who is able to take an outside perspective on their own culture and who is somewhat familiar with Western culture and communication styles. I was fortunate to find many people who were able to provide this kind of insight among my Chinese colleagues and students. It can be helpful to speak to other Foreign Teachers who have more experience living and working in China. However, evaluate their advice and insight carefully for bias and stereotyping. Again, this is a process that takes time and intentional involvement. Mistakes will be made, communication breakdowns will happen, but the effort will be worthwhile.

Role of teaching English in context

Another important aspect of teaching English in China is understanding the purpose for learning English. There are many types of institutions that offer English Language courses, usually for academic purposes, vocational purposes, or for passing exams to obtain certifications. The latter generally takes place in either an academic or vocational setting, but the style of teaching will be quite different. I will briefly list some of the common institutions that may employ Foreign Teachers and the kind of English language teaching they are expected to provide:

Schools (general public):

- Preschool or Kindergarten: familiarity with the language, native pronunciation, an interactive teaching style;
- Elementary school: English for exams, some conversational English, memorization and drills, performances such as singing or reciting vocabulary (very much driven by the need to show parents their children are learning something); more schools are adopting interactive teaching methods;
- Junior Middle School: exams take precedence; reading, writing, and listening exercises and tests are more common than oral English or interactive instruction; class sizes range from 30-90 students; some schools are adopting interactive language teaching methods;
- Senior Middle School: exams are most important, particularly the National Higher Education Entrance Exam and nearly all English language instruction becomes focused on increasing exam scores (which includes and English section); reading, writing and listening are most important, some schools include a speaking class; the third and final year of SMS is usually entirely devoted to test preparation and is usually the most difficult year in the entire Chinese education system;
- Vocational colleges: English for specific purposes; often more emphasis on spoken English and communication skills;
- Universities: academic English; some emphasis on spoken English skills depending on the major.

Language Training Centers:

- Academic test preparation: focus mainly on reading, writing, and listening to pass various exams for students or working professionals; for profit so student recruitment and retention is a top priority;
- International test preparation: focus on training students to pass exams for higher education such as SAT, TOEFL, IELTS; for profit so student recruitment and retention is a top priority;
- General language training: can have many different types of classes, but tend to balance reading, writing, listening and speaking; teachers are generally expected to entertain students and pressure is high to show student progress; for profit so student recruitment and retention is a top priority.

Additional Considerations

There is much more that could be discussed regarding English language teaching in China. However, there are a few more tips that would be helpful to know in preparation for teaching there. Remember that there are many variables that will influence specific teaching situations and students. In general I found the following to be true:

- Students were not accustomed to homework being very meaningful. They had largely been writing, reading, listening and sometimes speaking only for tests. This seemed to contribute to a lack of motivation to invest much effort into homework assignments. I found it helpful to explicitly tell students why they were doing an assignment and how they could make it a meaningful learning experience. The students responded well and tended to make better use of their homework assignments as learning opportunities. Giving specific feedback on how to improve was also crucial—and something most students had not gotten in previous language classes.
- Students were not accustomed to "fun" language learning exercises and tended to be more familiar with drilling and written exercises. Teaching methodology is changing in some areas so this also depends on students' educational background; most have not experienced learning through games or play so it can be helpful to explain purpose behind activities. In nearly every class I would have students who at first were very resistant to the idea that playing a game could be meaningful. However once the intent was explained, most students became enthusiastic participants. It is important to pay attention to student comfort level and realize that for many these kinds of activities will be new and unfamiliar.
- Students were generally accustomed to strongly authoritative teachers. I found that I needed to be more authoritative in a college classroom than I would have been teaching in the U.S. My students found my classes to be much more relaxed than their other courses and this sometimes led to overly casual attitudes. I had to learn when to remind students of my authority. Also students felt they were learning more when I maintained a more authoritarian position. All teachers will need to find their own balance and learn to balance what students expect with their own teaching style. Some expectations I noticed included:
    o Anticipation of strong discipline

- - Students often feared giving wrong answers or being scolded for mistakes
  - Teacher as expert – students were usually not accustomed to listening to each other and chose not to pay attention to one another. It was helpful to explicitly teach the value of peer interaction and feedback in language learning from the beginning of each of my courses. I also had to make sure that as the teacher, I was involved in interaction and feedback with each student regularly as well.
  - If there is not enough teacher talk time, students sometimes felt they were not learning enough. Here again it is important to help students understand the value of each part of the lesson. For students I was teaching for the first time, I would begin most courses with more direct instruction from me and then gradually increase the amount of student centered time. Keeping activities focused with clearly defined learning goals will also be important.
- Students were generally not accustomed to interactive language learning. Most had never used English outside of the classroom and so asking them to talk with each other, perform role plays, create dialogs, or play interactive games, was quite new. As mentioned already, it was important to explicitly teach the reasons for using the various activities. In addition, students needed more instruction on how to do each activity. I structured my courses so that interactive assignments increased in complexity and independent work on the part of the students so that by the end of the semester students were able to create entire plays, dialogs, or respond to impromptu role plays readily.

Teaching English in China was an experience that taught me more about myself, my own culture, and my own teaching philosophy than I had ever anticipated. I had many opportunities to learn that my assumptions about learning and teaching were culturally based and that I needed to adjust to fit the needs of my students. I greatly appreciated the patience and understanding from my administrators, colleagues and students as I learned to navigate a new culture. Teaching in a foreign culture is very challenging, but also rewarding and well worth the effort!

In this chapter, I presented to you with four narrative experiences from teachers who have taught in a variety of different contexts. It is important to note that even in one country, you will experience a diversity of requirements and situations. For this reason, in the next chapter, I provide you with principles for teaching practice that can support you, I hope, in any context in which you might find yourself.

7 GUIDING PRINCIPLES FOR TEACHING PRACTICE

In this chapter, I will present seven principles grounded in some of the theories we have discussed thus far that I hope will support the development of your own approach to teaching. The seven principles include: Understanding, Purpose, Connections, Engagement, Application, Assessment and Reflection. In the center of all of these principles is the active practice of action research, an empowering tool for teacher practitioners to support their own teaching practice. Note that these principles are not mutually exclusive as represented by the dotted lines. You will no doubt be continually shifting your teaching practice through ongoing assessments and reflections to inform your understanding of your student needs.

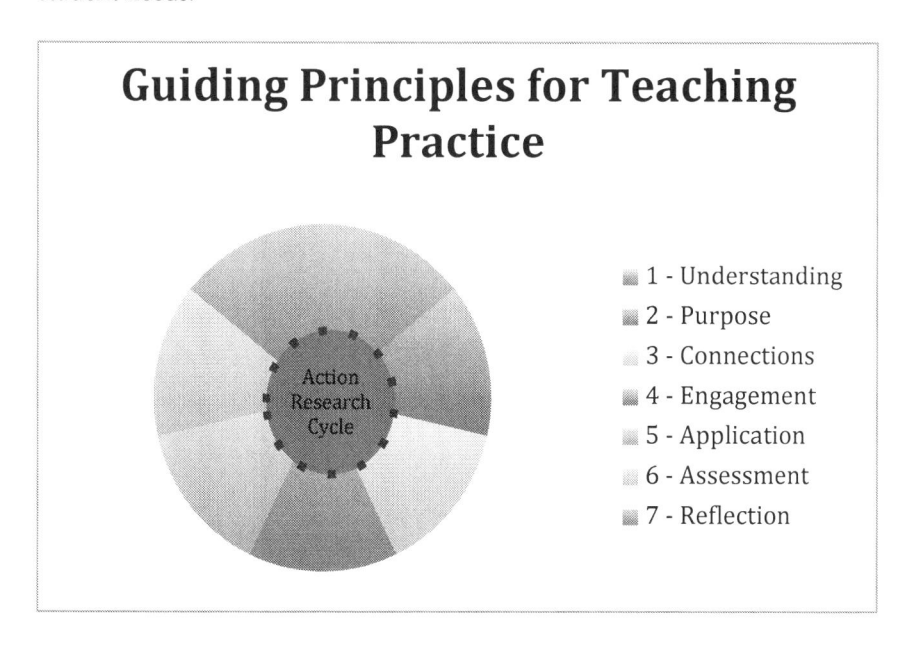

Guiding Principles for Teaching Practice

Action Research Cycle

- 1 - Understanding
- 2 - Purpose
- 3 - Connections
- 4 - Engagement
- 5 - Application
- 6 - Assessment
- 7 - Reflection

Principle 1: Understanding your context and your students

Before engaging in any curricular design, it is important to understand your terrain. Some guiding questions include:

- Who are you?
- What is the context of your school?
- Who are your students and what is their context?
- Why are they taking your course?
- What are their goals and how do they fit into the goals for the course?
- What are their interests and how can they be integrated into the course?
- What are their needs?

Who are you?

This is a very deeply philosophical question, but an important one to ask yourself. In relation to teaching, this would be a good time to stop and reflect on your own values, your beliefs about education and teaching, your reasons for coming to this profession, your beliefs about your own teaching practice and perceived impact, and your beliefs about your students. You also might want to be prepared for shifts to take place in your values, beliefs, and identities as you teach in various contexts and begin to interact with students, families and communities.

What is the context and culture of your school?

Before you go into the particular institution where you will work, conduct a little exploration of the mission, vision, values and goals of the school. Where is your school situated? To what extent does your school interact with the community that surrounds them? How is your school perceived by the community? Is your school a government or private school? If government or state school, then what curriculum or guidelines are mandated by the Ministry of Education, for example? How is student success measured at your school? What is the political structure of the school? Are other teachers open to having you observe them and learn alongside them? It is important to understand the wider context of your school to understand your position as you enter into the often unseen and unspoken social and political undercurrents of the school.

Who are your students and what is their context?

After understanding the wider context of the school and the community in which it resides, it is important to understand the reason for your presence in that school: your students. You may be able to find some information about your students from the previous inquiry on the context of the school, but it will be important for you to spend some time thinking about your own background and educational experiences and how they might be similar to or different from those of your students. You may want to study their culture if different from yours, and the educational history, traditional and contemporary approaches to teaching. Perhaps your students might come from very wealthy families where they have the luxuries of personal tutors and extra-curricular learning opportunities. On the other end of the spectrum, you may be working with students from homes where both parents work or the students work themselves and are unable to participate fully in the educational experience. Your students may have to take care of other siblings and tend to the needs of the family. You might have a wide array of different backgrounds in your classroom, but it is important to understand their context, not from your own lens, but from theirs, in order to develop relationships with them and adjust your teaching expectations and approach. For example, if you are in a cultural context with strict behavioral expectations for men and women and the interactions between unmarried gender are frowned upon, you may not want to integrate group activities that integrate men and women. If you were in a cultural context where teachers are seen as the center of the teaching-learning experience, you may not want to quickly push students into telling you what they would like to learn.

Why are they taking your course?

Understanding the reason why they are in your classroom is also very important. Is your class labeled as a lower level or higher level language class? Is this course a course that students have to take as part of the curriculum? Were they told to take the course or did they have a choice in the selection of the course as an elective? What perceptions do students have about your course? What will your course enable them to do after they successfully complete it? All of these aspects will play a role in their participation in your course.

What are their goals?

In addition to the goals and objectives set by the institution, it is also important to understand your student's goals. What do they want to do with increased proficiency in the English language? Do they want to be able to help their children with their homework? Do they want to come to the West for higher education? Do they want a better job? Knowing their goals can help you design your lesson or if you have a set curriculum, figure out creative ways in which to integrate their goals into your lesson.

What are their interests?

This question takes it to a more personal level of relationship development. What do they do in their spare time? Do they have special talents and skills? What do they like to read or watch on television? You can use this information for learning about their interests, generating content and meeting objectives of the course at the same time. Through this process, not only will you be able to create a bond with your students through having common topics to discuss, but they might be more inclined or motivated to study if the topic or theme is centered around their interests.

What are their needs?

If you are in the K-12 sector, then students are probably put into your classrooms by grade level. However, if you are teaching in English language programs, they may be leveled into your classrooms based on some form of assessment. You may want to obtain their institutional or standardized tests if available and conduct your own informal assessment to understand their current needs as your baseline data. You might also want to ask them what their thoughts are about their placement.

Principle 2: Mining for purpose

Sometimes teachers jump right into their lessons, but it is important to step back and consciously reflect on the purpose and goals of the lesson. Students benefit tremendously from knowing how each of their given tasks within a lesson contribute to a larger goal of the unit. Some guiding questions include:

- o What are the purpose and objectives of the program, your course and lesson?
- o How are you going to integrate macro-skill areas into your lessons?
- o What strategies can you employ in supporting and scaffolding student learning?
- o What should your students be able to do by the end of the lesson?

What are the objectives of your program, your course and lesson?

Understanding the purpose and objectives of your program and how that filters into your course and lesson is important because it shows you how your course fits into the overall program. It is important to understand the general framework both from a hierarchical or vertical perspective (your program -> your course -> your lesson), but also from a horizontal perspective.

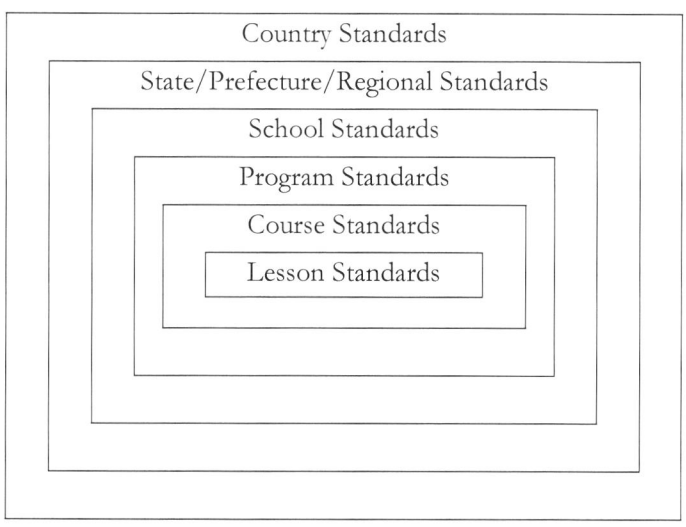

```
┌─────────────────────────────────────────────┐
│              Country Standards              │
│  ┌───────────────────────────────────────┐  │
│  │   State/Prefecture/Regional Standards │  │
│  │  ┌─────────────────────────────────┐  │  │
│  │  │        School Standards         │  │  │
│  │  │  ┌───────────────────────────┐  │  │  │
│  │  │  │     Program Standards     │  │  │  │
│  │  │  │  ┌─────────────────────┐  │  │  │  │
│  │  │  │  │   Course Standards  │  │  │  │  │
│  │  │  │  │  ┌───────────────┐  │  │  │  │  │
│  │  │  │  │  │Lesson Standards│ │  │  │  │  │
│  │  │  │  │  └───────────────┘  │  │  │  │  │
│  │  │  │  └─────────────────────┘  │  │  │  │
│  │  │  └───────────────────────────┘  │  │  │
│  │  └─────────────────────────────────┘  │  │
│  └───────────────────────────────────────┘  │
└─────────────────────────────────────────────┘
```

Figure 2. Organizational Schema on Language Teaching

If there are several programs in your institution, what are the differences between them and do any of the programs feed into one another? If students matriculate into your program from another program, what were the exit requirements for that program? In your program, if there are multiple sections of the same course, it might be helpful to understand how other teachers are approaching their courses. Are you all provided a uniform curriculum and syllabus? Are you free to generate your own? What opportunities are there to share ideas and discuss concerns with instructors teaching the same courses? If there are multiple levels of writing classes, what are the exit requirements for the previous level? What are the expectations of the teachers in the level beyond yours so that you can support your students in developing skills required for that level?

Levels					
Level 5					
Level 4					
Level 3 (01)	Level 3 (02)	Level 3 (03)	Level 3 (04)	Level 3 (05)	*Sections (eg. Writing)*
Level 2					
Level 1					

Figure 3. Vertical and Horizontal Continuums of Courses within Programs

These conversations between teachers are important so that you can do your best to support student learning so that they can be successful at the next level.

How are you going to integrate macro-skill areas into your lessons?

Based on the focus of your program, you may be required to follow a grammatical syllabus, which is focused grammar structures such as learning the past tense forms of verbs, a task-based syllabus, which focuses on language through the carrying out of tasks such as planning an event, a notional functional syllabus, which focuses on functions of the language within a particular context such as ordering food at a restaurant, or content-based syllabus focused on language instruction within particular content areas such as science and history. In another program, you may be given a course on one of the macro-skill areas of language such as reading, writing, listening, and speaking or an integrated skills course. You may also be given a stand-alone course to teach on TOEFL (Test of English as a Foreign Language), Conversation Class or Academic Vocabulary, and possible vocational courses such as English for Mechanics, English for Business, English for Nursing, or English for Engineering. It is not possible for any certification program to provide you with all of the possibilities, but it is important to approach teaching from a holistic perspective. Using the principles as a guidepost, research the course you are going to be teaching and look for ways in which you can integrate the four macro-skill areas into your lessons.

What strategies can you employ in supporting and scaffolding student learning?

It is important to have a bag of tools you can use in supporting student learning, but use them if it meets your learning objectives. Critical application is necessary, otherwise, your lesson can have a myriad of activities, but your students might not have met the objectives of your lesson. If the focus of your lesson is student learning, then think of step-by-step approach of designing and employing a series of tasks that would scaffolding the learning process for your students in order to help them reach the objectives. For example, you may want to use a think-pair-share activity for students to begin making connections between what they know and what they are about to learn. You may want to use graphic organizers to help them brainstorm ideas and organize their thoughts in preparation for a writing assignment. You may want students to jigsaw a reading so that they can help each other break down the concepts and allow for more input and output opportunities to support them in their language development. There are many such tools you can use in the language classroom no matter what course you are offered to teach, but it is important to put careful thought into the rationale for employing these strategies, the sequencing of these strategies within the lesson where one strategy builds on the previous one, the time it will take to carry out the strategies and the cognitive and linguistic appropriateness of the strategies.

What should your students be able to do by the end of the lesson/course?

It is also important to consider the end goal of your lesson and backward plan to the various components you will include in your lesson to help your students meet the objectives. For example, if by the end of your lesson you want your students to be able to write an introduction, you may backward plan by thinking about the placement of direct instruction activities, group work, and individual work within your lesson so that students have a completed introduction by the end of the lesson. For a course that is allotted 90 minutes, you may want to spend the first 20 minutes covering the three components of a paragraph; namely the hook, background information, and thesis. You might want to share model introductions written by students in your previous classes to serve as mentor texts. You may want them to evaluate some sample introductions for quality of the hook, background information and thesis statement. For the next 30 minutes, you can invite students to write their own paragraphs based on the instructions and models they received. You can provide them with a graphic organizer with the three segments indicated. Then, for the next 15 minutes, you can pair students up and have them engage in peer review, where they review the quality of each other's hooks, background information, and thesis statements. They could support each other with clarifying their ideas or making the introductions more interesting. For the final 25 minutes, students can work on revising their own introductions. Based on student levels and the culture of the classroom, you might find that the timing provided here does not work. Again, time is dependent on your student needs. The allocation of time for this lesson was just for the purpose of illustration. In order to know whether or not your students have met the objectives for your lesson, you can review their completed introductions at the end of the class and determine what you will review in the next class based on their needs.

Principle 3: Connecting current with new knowledge

Building background and bridging are concepts that have been drawn upon in student-centered classrooms where students are used as the starting point of the lesson rather than the textbook or prescribed curriculum. Given this, knowing where students current level of understanding is based on their experiences and background can help to serve as a foundation in integrating new knowledge into their existing systems. Some guiding questions include:

- What background knowledge and experiences do your students already have regarding the upcoming topic?
- What language knowledge do they already have?

What background knowledge and experiences do your students already have regarding the upcoming topic?

It is as important for you to ascertain your background knowledge as much as it is important to find out your student's background knowledge on the subject you are about to teach. If your program has provided you with a text and the content area is Business English, you may not come to the course with the background knowledge necessary to teach the course. However, you can study the concepts ahead of time and solicit knowledge from your students and other experts in the field who can come to your class and present on particular topics within the field of Business English. Remember that you are the facilitator of the learning process and can learn alongside your students as well. If your upcoming topic was going to be about the weather, it might be helpful to find out what weathers your students have experienced. Have they gone to the beach? Have they experienced the desert? Have they experienced snow? Learning about the background experiences and knowledge of your students can help you refrain from making assumptions and help to more accurately bridge their prior learning to the new content. This is an example from my own personal experience. Once in a conversation with my now husband, he made reference to a popular American television program, Flipper. In seeing that I had no reaction to his joke, he could not understand why, and made the following remark. "I can't believe you don't know Flipper. How can you not know Flipper?" To this, I reacted, "Do you know Dorae-mon?" Dorae-mon is a famous Japanese cartoon that all children who grow up in Japan know. My husband of course did not know Dorae-mon and began to understand his own assumptions about my cultural knowledge.

What language knowledge do they already have?

In thinking about language as both building blocks, but also holistically, what are the language patterns, grammar structures, vocabulary, skills your students already have? What did they learn in the previous course that you can build on in your course? How can you take the previous lesson and build on the learning form that lesson to slowly increase your student proficiency levels in their areas of need. If your students have really strong reading and writing skills, but are not as proficient in their listening and speaking skills, how can you integrate more speaking and listening activities to support them in developing those skills. If you are teaching a listening and speaking course and your students require more development in their reading and writing skills, you can integrate reading and writing activities into their listening and speaking course by having them read a play and enact it, or write a poem or story and dramatize it.

Principle 4: Engaging in active learning

Unless learners are actively participating in the learning process, they will not acquire language. Therefore, it is important to carefully select tasks that are of interest to the students and are at the student's cognitive and slightly above their proficiency level, providing a balanced interplay between comfort and challenge. Some guiding questions include:

- What interactive tasks will you set up to engage your learners in actively participating in the learning process?
- How will you ensure that all students are engaged in the learning process?

What interactive tasks will you set up to engage your learners in actively participating in the learning process?

There are many types of interactions that can take place in the classroom. Students can actively engage and interact with their texts, with their peers, and with you, as their teacher. In moving away from the teacher-fronted classroom to the student-centered classroom, given that the cultural context in which you find yourself approves this type of approach, you may want to think about how you can talk less and the students can talk more, i.e. how your role can be minimized and theirs can be empowered to take charge of their own learning. Your primarily role will be setting up the tasks and coming up with contingency plans, but then handing over the learning process to your students. Will you have them engage in group work? Will they be in same level grouping or different level groupings? Will you have them in groups of two, three, four or more? If so, what is the rationale for your decision?

How will you ensure that all students are engaged in the learning process?
It is quite common in group work for students with higher proficiency levels or outgoing personalities to take charge of the group and speak on behalf of the group. In order to ensure that all students participate equally, you will have to assign roles and tasks that each member of the group will be responsible for completing the task. Some examples of this include the literature circles, information gap, and jigsaw activities.

Principle 5: Applying learning to current and other contexts

Because knowledge is not an isolated and static phenomena, it is important for teachers to explicitly link the application of the knowledge to other contexts so that students can understand that the skills they are learning in your lesson or course could be applicable to other areas within the class and beyond the classroom. Some guiding questions include:

- What opportunities will you provide your students to practice the knowledge they have acquired in this lesson?
- What opportunities will you provide students to apply their knowledge to other situations or contexts?

What opportunities will you provide your students to practice the knowledge they have acquired in this lesson?

What tasks will you line up within your lesson so students can apply their knowledge. For example, in the previous lesson on writing introductions, after teaching them about writing effective hooks, including relevant background knowledge and writing clear thesis statements, students had opportunities to look at mentor texts and evaluate the three components of an introduction, they got to write their own introductions, they got to evaluate their peer's introductions and provide suggestions for improvement and then they got to revise their introductions again before submitting it to the teacher. They were allowed multiple opportunities to practice and apply their knowledge.

What opportunities will you provide students to apply their knowledge to other situations or contexts?

When students learn content, it is important to provide them opportunities to demonstrate their acquisition of the content not only within the lesson, but beyond the lesson. For example, if they learned about making arguments for and against a particular topic of opinion or argumentative papers in their writing class, how can this knowledge be applied to other courses? For example, they can have a debate about the topic they wrote about in their conversation class. Here again, it is important for teachers to collaborate with one another on the learning objectives for their students. The more opportunities they have to practice and apply their knowledge in different contexts, the deeper their learning will be. After practicing it in the classrooms, you might want to invite other stakeholders as panelists who might find the topic of interest, particularly if it is an area of interest for the school. Exploring potential transference of knowledge and skills to other contexts and sharing that with your students could be beneficial as they will begin to see the broader context in which their language skills and efforts in developing their language skills can be utilized.

Principle 6: Assessing their learning

It is important to know how we know what we know. In other words, we need to back up our conclusions about our teaching and student learning with some evidence. This means assessment – assessment can be formal or informal. Formal assessment often include quizzes and tests. Informal assessments can include observational data as you listen in on group work for example, or reviewing student artifacts such as their written pieces, group posters, or presentations. What I find most useful is a combination of both formal and informal assessments. Some guiding questions include:

- o How do you know that your students met the learning objectives for the lesson?
- o What forms of assessment (formal or informal) are you using to document their learning of the objectives?

How do you know that your students met the learning objectives for the lesson/course?

It is important to identify the end goals of your lesson/course and tie it back to your objectives for the lesson. What should they be able to do by the end of the lesson/course? Were they able to meet the objectives? How do you know? It is important to always come back to the original intent of your course and lesson to see if your plan supported student learning of the objectives.

What forms of assessment (formal or informal) are you using to document their learning of the objectives?

There are two types of assessments. One is formal assessments in the form of quizzes, tests, oral exams, or written papers. Others are informal assessments including your own observations of your teaching and student learning by orally checking for comprehension, walking around the room and listening in on group discussions, or having students submit exit evaluations at the end of class where they respond to particular questions you pose or record what they have learned that day. It is important to have continual assessments known as "formative assessments" to improve your own teaching practice, which will then further support student learning, rather than one final summative assessment, conducted only at the end of the lesson or the term. At the end of the lesson, you still have opportunities to make changes for the following lesson, but at the end of the course, there really is no value because there is nothing you can do about it at that point. By the end of the course, you should have a pretty good idea about each student's development. If their end of course performance comes as a surprise, there must have been some indication during that might have contributed to this discrepancy.

Principle 7: Reflecting on my teaching and student learning

Reflection is such an integral part of teaching practice that happens at all stages of the principles delineated. It is important to constantly reflect before, during and after the lesson and course. For example, if students are not able to understand the task at hand, it is important to stop and rephrase in the moment. You have to develop flexibility and adapt to the ever-changing needs of your students.

- o What went well in your lesson/course?
- o What did not go so well in your lesson/course and how did you adapt to the changing needs of your students in the moment?
- o What were your students able to do? What do they still need to work on?
- o What did you learn about yourself and your teaching

> practice?
> - What would you do differently next time? Why?

What went well in your lesson/course?

After the lesson is completed, it is important to go back and reflect on what went well in the lesson before embarking on planning and developing the next lesson. Likewise, at the end of your course, after completing all of the final assessments and submitting grades, it's important to take a look at student evaluations and look for areas that you did well in first rather than dive into areas of concern. I think as teachers, we are often so hard on ourselves that it is important for us to stop and take a look at what we also do well.

What did not go so well in your lesson/course and how did you adapt to the changing needs of your students in the moment?

After commending ourselves on what we do well, we can take a look at the areas of our lesson/course that did not go as planned. As we analyze and seek answers to this, it might be a good time to invite other instructors, as well as your own students to inquire as to how you can go about improving these areas. Some might be as simple as to take out a few assignments because the number of assignments were overwhelming for the students and were not necessary in order to demonstrate the skills required to meet the student learning objectives. It might be related to providing more time for particular concepts. Other areas that require improvement may take more time such as observing other teachers who are successful in teaching a particular concept, consulting research or attending conferences on a particular theme. The point being, we are constantly evolving as teachers and we need to be good to ourselves, but conscious of our areas of strength as well as areas that require further development. Instead of hiding these unpleasant areas, it is important to come to terms with them and seek the support of your colleagues, mentors, and administration.

Teachers as Practitioner Researchers: The tool of action research

Theorists in the field of TESOL have recognized the value of action research in teacher development (Crookes, 1993; Burns, 2000). However, there has also been some criticism regarding the practice of Action Research. For example, though the philosophy of action research is to empower the teacher, power differentials appear to still exist, where the teacher takes on a secondary role to the researchers whether it be through reading research and valuing research findings as being more important than their own understanding of their students and their classroom experience, or through working with a professor (Kumaravadivelu, 2012). In the approach to action research I take here, I would like to put the teacher and his or her students as the central unit where decisions about what happens in that classroom are made. Rather than attempting to consult articles and follow prescribed methods developed by theorists, I encourage you to develop your own teaching practice based on the needs of your students and in consultation with your fellow teachers, mentor teachers, and community members in a forum similar to that of a professional learning communities focused on student learning (Dufor, 2004). The central focus of these professional learning communities could be the process of dialogizing. Dialogizing, is a very complex term, with multiple dimensions (Freire, 1970; Wells, 1999; Bahktin, 1981; Kumaravadivelu, 2012). In essence, dialogizing is a process whereby people come together without the imposition of power dimensions, to explore issues through authentic conversations with the goal of learning, of shifting one's views, and of transforming one's self.

Given this frame, rather than taking research findings or curriculum and directly apply them in your teaching, analyze these ideas in your learning communities and reflect on their applicability in your classrooms. Will these ideas support student learning? How do you know? Implement the ideas in your classroom and assess your student learning of the concepts through informal and formal means. Present the data from your class to your colleagues and engage in deep discussions about what was assessed, how it was assessed, what does the data really mean, does the data really reflect student learning, how can you adapt your assessments to truly reflect student learning, and how can improve student learning of these concepts in the next lesson? Most importantly, it is important to understand that action research is a cyclical process and does not end after one cycle; it continues on to help you improve your educational practice. If you want to engage in teacher research, here are some guiding questions.

The Action Research Cycle
1. What concern/issue/problem/question do I currently have in my classroom?
2. Can I do anything about this concern/issue/problem/question?
3. What does the research say about my concern/issue/problem/question? What do my colleagues, mentors, students have to say about my concern/issue/problem?
4. What is my action plan based on my research, consultation and understanding of the concern/issue/problem/question?

5. After implementing my action plan, was my concern/issue/problem/question addressed or improved?
6. What were the results of my formal and informal assessments? Did I have other data points that I could use to inform my understanding of the results of my action plan? For example, did I consult with a colleague and have her observe my class? Did I take notes? Did I audio or video-record my sessions to observe my class? Did I interview or survey my students about their own learning?
7. After reviewing the various data points and consulting with colleagues and mentors about the data, what else can I do to address my concern/issue/problem/question?
8. Upon reflection, what is my new, revised, or more specified concern/issue/problem/question?
9. What is my action plan based on my research, consultation and understanding of the concern/issue/problem/question?

*** *Continue progressing through the cycle from 6-9 until your find some resolution.*

10. Overall reflections and conclusions on your learning from this action research process about your concern/issue/problem/question and developing a new area of concern/issue/problem/question you would like to embark on for your next project.

In this chapter, I presented a set of guiding principles to support your approach and teaching practice in any content area or context in which you will teach. Because they are not prescribed methods, it allows you the flexibility to adapt to the ever changing needs of the context in which you will find yourself and the students to whom you will serve. I hope the seven principles and action research tool presented here guide you in your thinking process in developing and designing curricular materials, but also in thinking about and reflecting on your teaching practice throughout your teaching career.

8 CONCLUSION

In my own experience, I have found that working in multiple settings has not only expanded my understanding of the field, but also helped me to adapt and be flexible to the changing landscape of the field. For example, as an undergraduate student, during my breaks I would go to Japan for the summers to visit my family and would take on teaching positions as an assistant to a classroom teacher in my former international school. This transitioned into myself becoming a classroom teacher after a few years for a combined 1st and 2nd grade classroom. The focus at this school was using English as medium of instruction for content area courses such as math, science, and history. During my time in college, I also began to teach Japanese as a foreign language at an elementary school and also as a beginning level Japanese instructor for a University in Honolulu. At the elementary level, I taught the children vocabulary words related to particular themes, but mostly taught them an appreciation for the Japanese culture. At the university level beginning Japanese course, I was provided a textbook and curriculum to follow, so I integrated my ideas and activities within the framework provided.

When I moved to California, I got a position teaching English to a beginning level class in a noncredit program at a community college, and slowly took on a variety of different levels. I then moved into credit bearing English classes that focused on specific macro-skill areas such as reading, writing, listening, and speaking. I taught vocabulary and grammar courses as stand-alone courses and also some integrated skills courses as I continued to learn while teaching. I also worked at a language academy associated with a university with international students from a variety of countries. In this context, I prepared them for college-readiness and worked on developing critical thinking, reading, and writing skills.

One summer, I taught a group of migrant students in a second story of a church. The classroom was dimly lit, with very limited resources. While I had a variety of different resources and technology in some of the other settings, on the second story of the church I went back to basics with one marker and a small white board and taught the multi-level needs of those students. If I have to share with you my most inspiring group of students, this was it. These students worked long and hard days in the heat of the summer on different farms, but would get cleaned up for class every evening at 6 p.m. We would work from 6-10 p.m. on Mondays through Thursdays. We had one project for the whole class, but the writing required differed based on their proficiency levels. For some students, I began working with the alphabet to teach them how to write their names. Others, who were literate in their first language and had some foundation in the English language, were able to write paragraphs. At the end of the term, I compiled all of their written work, pictures and images of themselves and what they valued in their lives into a class book, with all of their stories and histories combined. They were able to take these home and share them with their families.

Such experiences have really informed my teaching practice. Particularly, my understanding that one method or approach is not going to meet the needs of all of these students. Rather, as you read in this book and were introduced to the variety of methods, principles and approaches, continue to bear in mind the role of English within the context in which you will teach as a backdrop, and how this understanding can inform your selection of appropriate teaching materials, methods and approaches reflective of the needs and goals within your particular context.

REFERENCES

Alsagoff, L, McKay, S. L., Hu,G., & Renandya, W. A. (2012). *Principles and practices for teaching English as an international language.* New York: Routledge.

Asher, J. (1969). The total physical response approach to second language learning. *The Modern Language Journal, 53*(1), 3-17.

Ausubel, D. (1962). A subsumption theory of meaningful verbal learning and retention. *The Journal of General Psychology, 66* (2), 213-224.

Bakhtin, M. (1981). *The dialogic imagination: Four essays.* Austin, TX: University of Texas Press.

Bloom B. S. (1956). *Taxonomy of Educational Objectives, Handbook I: The Cognitive Domain.* New York: David McKay Co Inc.

Brown, D. (2007). *Principles of language learning and teaching.* New York, NY: Longman, Inc.

Burns, A. *Participatory action research and ESL.* New York: Cambridge University Press.

Canale, M. (1983). From communicative competence to communicative language pedagogy. In Richards, J. C., & Schmidt, R. W. (Eds.), *Language and Communication*, (pp. 2-27), London: Longman.

Canale, M. & Swain, M. (1980). Theoretical bases of communicative approach to second language teaching and testing. *Applied Linguistics,* 1, 1-47.

Chomsky, N. (1967). Review of Skinner's verbal behavior. In Jakobovits & Miron (Eds.), *Readings in the Psychology of Language,* (pp. 142-143), Upper Saddle River, NJ: Prentice Hall, Inc.

Corder, S.P. (1967). The significance of learners' errors. *IRAL,* 5, 161-170.

Crookes, G. (1993). Action research for SL teachers – going beyond teacher research. *Applied Linguistics, 14* (2), 130-144.

Crystal, D. (1997). *English as a global language*. Cambridge: Cambridge University Press.

Daniels, H. (1994). *Literature Circles: Voice and Choice in the Student-Centered Classroom*. Markham: Pembroke Publishers Ltd.

Dufor, R. (2004). What is a professional learning community? *Educational Leadership, 61* (8), 6-11.

Freire, P. (1970) *Pedagogy of the Oppressed*. New York: Continuum Books.

Fries, C. C. (1952). The structure of English: An introduction to the construction of English sentences. New York: Harcourt, Brace.

Gass, S. M. (2013). *Second language acquisition: An introductory course* (4th ed.). New York, NY: Routledge.

Gattegno, Caleb (1963). *Teaching foreign languages in schools: The silent way* (1st ed.). Reading, UK: Educational Explorers.

Gibbons, P. (2002). *Scaffolding language, scaffolding learning: Teaching second language learners in the mainstream classroom*. Portsmouth, NH: Heinemann.

Gooman, K. S. (1967). Reading: A psycholinguistic game. *Journal of the Reading Specialist 6*, 126-135.

Hymes, D. H. (1971). Competence and performance in linguistic theory. In R. Huxley & E. Ingram (Eds.), *Language acquisition: Model and methods* (pp. 3-28). New York: Academic Press.

Krashen, S. (1981), *Second language acquisition and second language learning*, Oxford: Pergamon Press.

Krashen, S. (1982), *Principles and practice in second language acquisition*, Oxford: Pergamon Press.

Krashen, S. D. & Terrell, T. D. (1983, 1996). *The natural approach: Language acquisition in the classroom*. Northumberland, UK: Bloodaxe Books, Ltd.

Kumaravadivelu, B. (1994). The postmethod condition: (E)merging strategies for second/foreign language. *TESOL Quarterly, 28* (1), 27-48.

Kumaravadivelu, B. (2006). *Teaching from method to postmethod.* Mahwah, NJ: Lawrence Erlbaum Associates Publishers.

Kumaravadivelu, B. (2012). *Language teacher education for a global society.* New York: Routledge.

Laresen-Freeman, D. (2000). *Techniques and principles in language teaching.* (2nd ed.) Oxford: Oxford University Press.

Larsen-Freeman, D. & Anderson, M. (2011). *Techniques and principles in language teaching.* (3rd ed.) Oxford: Oxford University Press.

Lenneberg, E.H. (1967). *Biological foundations of language.* Hoboken, NJ: Wiley.

Mackey, A. (2002). Beyond production: learners' perceptions about interactional processes. *International Journal of Educational Research, 37* (3-4), 379-394.

McKay, S. L. (1992). *Teaching English overseas: An introduction.* Oxford: Oxford University Press.

McKay, S. L. (2002). *Teaching English as an international language.* Oxford: Oxford University Press.

McKay, S. L. & Bokhorst-Heng, W. D. (2008). *International English in its sociolinguistic context.* New York: Routledge.

Molina, S. C. (2013). *Linguistics for teaching English in multilingual classrooms.* Charleston, SC: CreateSpace.

Piaget, J. (1970). *Main trends in psychology. London, UK:* Allen & Unwin, Ltd.

Position statement on English as a global language http://www.tesol.org/docs/pdf/10884 Teachers of English to Speakers of Other Languages, Inc. A Global Education Association Founded in 1966. Obtained from the world wide web on October 9th, 2013.

Raman, M. (2005). *English language teaching.* New Delhi, India: Atlantic Publishers & Distributors Pvt. Ltd.

Roberge, M. (2007, April). Language minority students in college English. *Miracosta College Lecture*. Lecture conducted from Miracosta College, Oceanside, CA.

Rogers, Carl R. (1969). *Freedom to learn: A view of what education might become*. Columbus, Ohio: Merrill Publishing Company.

Savignon, S. J. (1991). Communicative language teaching: State of the art. *TESOL Quarterly, 25*(2), 261-277.

Sinclair, J. M., & Coulthard, M. (1975). Towards an analysis of discourse: The English used by teachers and pupils. London: Oxford University Press.

Skinner, B. F. (1957). *Verbal behavior*. Acton, MA: Copley Publishing Group.

Swain, M. (1985). Communicative competence: Some roles of comprehensible input and comprehensible output in its development. In S. Gass & C. Madden (Eds.), *Input in second language acquisition* (pp. 235-253). Cambridge, MA: Newbury House.

Swain, C. (1995). Three functions of output in second language learning. In G. Cook and B. Seidlhofer (eds.), *Principle and Practice in Applied Linguistics: Studies in Honour of H.G. Widdowson* (pp. 125-144), Oxford University Press, Oxford.

Swain, M. & Lapkin, S. (1995). Problems in output and the cognitive processes they generate: A step towards second language learning. *Applied Linguistics* 16: 371-391.

Vygotsky, L. S. (1978). *Mind in society*. Cambridge, MA: Harvard University Press.

Wallace, C. (2001). Reading. In R. Carter and D. Nunan (eds.). *The Cambridge Guide to Teaching English to Speakers of Other Languages* (pp. 21-27). Cambridge, UK: Cambridge University Press.

Wells, G. (1999). *Dialogic inquiry: Towards a sociocultural practice and theory of education* Cambridge, UK: Cambridge University Press.

Widdowson, H. G. (1990). *Aspects of language teaching*. Oxford, UK: Oxford University Press.

ABOUT THE AUTHOR

Sarina Chugani Molina currently serves as faculty in the Department of Learning and Teaching at the University of San Diego. She has experience working with English Learners from a multitude of backgrounds both within the United States and in International contexts. She is the program coordinator and instructor of graduate level courses in the M.Ed. in TESOL, Literacy, and Culture Program. She has authored English as a Foreign Language textbooks series entitled, *Visual English* and most recently, *English for Global Citizens*. Her research interests include teacher development in TESOL, teaching English as a global language, and addressing social and educational inequities for students from culturally and linguistically diverse backgrounds.

Made in the USA
San Bernardino, CA
05 February 2020